PERSPECTIVES ON PORNOGRAPHY

Perspectives on Pornography

Sexuality in Film and Literature

Edited by
Gary Day *and* Clive Bloom

St. Martin's Press   New York

First published in the United States of America in 1988

Printed in Hong Kong

ISBN 0–312–01873–8

Library of Congress Cataloging-in-Publication Data
Perspectives on pornography: sexuality in film and literature
edited by Gary Day and Clive Bloom.
p.   cm.
Includes index.
ISBN 0–312–01873–8: $35.00 (est.)
1. Sex in literature.   2. Sex in motion pictures.   3. Pornography.
I. Day, Gary, 1956–.   II. Bloom, Clive.
PN56.S5P47   1988
809'.933538—dc19   88–4539
                                                          CIP

Contents

Preface and Acknowledgements

This volume provides a forum for a male–female dialogue concerning the history, dissemination and consequences of pornographic representation, with particular reference to pornography and eroticism in literature and film. The topic is one fraught with moral, political and sexual tensions, which the contributors tackle from a range of contemporary theoretical perspectives, such as feminism, post-structuralism, Marxism, Lacanian psychoanalysis and film theory. In so doing they challenge established views and seek to open doors for further exploration and debate.

The editors would like to thank Jane Gibb, Keith Shand, Lesley Bloom, Hazel Day, Graham Eyre, Carol Diethe and Frances Arnold for all their help and encouragement.

G. D. and C. B.

Notes on the Contributors

Alison Assiter teaches Philosophy at Thames Polytechnic. She has published numerous articles and is the author of *Pornography and Feminism*.

Clive Bloom is Coordinator of American Studies at Middlesex Polytechnic. He is General Editor of the Insights series and is the author of two books, *The 'Occult' Experience and the New Criticism* and *Reading Poe, Reading Freud: The Romantic Imagination in Crisis*.

Laura Claridge is Assistant Professor of English at the United States Naval Academy in Annapolis, Maryland. She is a frequent speaker at conferences and has published widely on feminist issues. She is currently working on a book, *The Paradox of Desire*, and is co-editor of *Male Feminist Voices*.

Anthony Crabbe teaches History of Art and Design at Trent Polytechnic. His research interests include Cubism and Purism and he is currently writing a book on the philosophical concept of time.

Gary Day is a member of the Graduate Centre of Middlesex Polytechnic. He is writing his doctoral thesis on Dickens. He has published various articles and poetry.

Carol Diethe is a lecturer in German at Middlesex Polytechnic. She is currently translating *Mafarka le futuriste* by F. Marinetti.

Richard Ellis teaches English and American Literature and Cultural Studies at North Staffordshire Polytechnic. He has published a number of articles on critical theory in practice.

Maggie Humm is Coordinator of Women's Studies at North East London Polytechnic. She has published a number of articles and essays on a wide range of feminist issues. She is also a member of Network, which represents women teaching in the humanities.

Avis Lewallen studied English at North London Polytechnic and is currently completing an MA in Women's Studies at the University of Kent. She has contributed an article on pornography in popular fiction to *The Female Gaze*.

Michael Woolf teaches literature at Tottenham College of Technology and writes on cultural matters for BBC Radio 4.

1
Introduction
GARY DAY

It is not often that men and women are found discussing in the same volume the topics of pornography and sexuality. Up till now, with one or two exceptions, most of the commentary and analysis has come from feminists such as Dworkin, Griffin, Carter, Cowie, Kuhn and Mulvey, whose writings have greatly extended our awareness of these topics. This book, although it shows the influence of these and other writers, is a new departure in the sense that it is a dialogue between men and women about pornography and sexuality in film and literature. It is not a manifesto or a programme for action but offers instead a number of perspectives, sometimes complementary, sometimes contradictory, on these and related issues. Since it does not stand for any one position, it is possible that parts of the book may enrage, but the aim rather is through this diversity to enlarge understanding about the representation of sexuality in film and literature.

The book is divided into three broad sections: 'Historical', 'Theoretical' and 'Critical'. There is, of course, considerable overlap between these areas, but such distinctions are useful in a general way as a means of organising the discussion.

The historical section contains three chapters. The first, by Clive Bloom (Chapter 2), tries to account for the failure of the Attorney General's Commission on Pornography to recommend any effective measures against the pornographic industry. Bloom shows that the Committee unwittingly sabotaged its conclusions by trying to apprehend a human essence through a mechanistic apparatus and he gives a historical account of how this situation arose.

Chapter 3, by Richard Ellis, is a scholarly and well-researched piece concentrating on the cut and thrust of courtroom battles as publishers fought for the right to make books banned for their sexual content available to the public. Ellis argues that the resulting process of decensorship was due not to any liberalisation or relaxation of the social *mores*, but rather to the growing perception

1

that sex could be used to enhance the selling power of a whole variety of products, thus strengthening the capitalist system. Given this context, Ellis claims, it seemed absurd not to publish books such as *Lady Chatterley's Lover* and *The Naked Lunch*. Anthony Crabbe picks up this point when he argues, in Chapter 4, that feature-length sex films have been made not to stimulate people to enlarge their sexual horizons but precisely to prevent them from doing so, lest the wheels of commerce should grind to a halt as people discovered a sensuous, more fulfilling lifestyle. Crabbe's article also raises some interesting speculations about pornography and erotica, female pleasure and why men watch sex films, and, as such, it leads into the theoretical section.

The first essay here (Chapter 5) is by Maggie Humm, who draws attention to the limitations of those theoretical approaches to representations of sexuality in film which concentrate on the gaze. Her argument is that, if feminists are to make an effective intervention into film criticism and are to develop a female erotica, then they must take into account the verbal as well as the visual aspects of films. My own essay (Chapter 6) is a psychoanalytic approach to pornography and attempts to show that the obvious-ness of the pornographic image can often mislead us as to its real significance. Alison Assiter (Chapter 7) asks whether popular romantic fiction is porn for women, since the heroines of these novels are objectified. She goes on to say that women contribute to their own oppression by reading this kind of literature, but she notes that its attention to the details of everyday life allows women to identify with the sexual life of the heroines, thereby gaining an erotic pleasure which offers them some compensation for the way patriarchy oppresses their real erotic life.

In the critical section Mike Woolf (Chapter 8) and Laura Claridge (Chapter 9) both take recognised works of literature and scrutinise their treatment of sexuality. Mike Woolf compares Kate Millett's *Flying* and Henry Miller's *Tropic of Cancer* and *Tropic of Capricorn* and poses the interesting paradox that, while in one respect sex in these works is seen as a release of the essential self from its ideological prison, in another it surrounds that self with various compulsions and obsessions, making it no more free than it was before. Laura Claridge gives a feminist account of Pope's *Rape of the Lock* and shows that Belinda escapes Pope's attempts to define her sexuality, thereby revealing the limitations of *male* sexuality. In Chapter 10 Avis Lewallen looks at the socialist–feminist writer

Angela Carter, and, though she approves of Carter's attempt to give a more realistic picture of female sexuality, she takes issue with her over her recommendation that women should be more sexually aggressive, since that only reinforces the dualism of power and powerlessness which Lewallen sees as lying at the root of the current problems of sexuality. Lewallen also criticises Carter for choosing, in *The Bloody Chamber*, to re-present female sexuality through the form of the fairytale, for, as she argues, the inherent stereotypical features of the form greatly inhibit any attempt to say something new through it. In the final chapter (11), Carol Diethe compares Marinetti's *Mafarka le futuriste* with Nietzsche's *Thus Spoke Zarathustra*, and argues that the former is pornographic to the extent that it presents women as accepting, and even enjoying, the abuse and violence which the protagonist inflicts upon them.

The question arises of what pattern, if any, emerges from all this. Broadly speaking, the men in the volume tend to take a more historical approach to the problem of sexual representation while the women tend to treat it as a matter requiring urgent attention in the present. It could be argued that, by choosing to write from a historical point of view, the men are in some way distancing themselves from current problems and that this distancing takes three forms. First, it is a covert denial that the current oppressed state of women has anything to do with the male sex; it is simply a matter of 'history' (the irony of *his* story of course goes unnoticed). Secondly, the historical approach absolves men of the need to act: history will resolve the problems in the same way as it caused them – silently, invisibly, inevitably – and only future historians will be able to see how it was done. Finally, the historical approach implies, ideally, a process of objectivity which is not dissimilar to the objectification which feminists see not just in pornography but in the representations of women in society generally. The historical approach could, then, be described as less an analysis than an apology for non-action – a fault from which my own contribution is not free.

However, although the historical approach has its disadvantages and may reveal, when employed by men, a disturbing kinship to some of the characteristics of pornography (e.g. the historical as over and done with, so that it appears fixed and natural like the presentation of sexuality in a pornographic film or magazine), it is not something that feminism should overlook, since its selection of pornography as a target is largely a matter of historical determination. It is not just that feminists are simply appalled by the grossness of pornography; it is rather that, as women, they are socially constructed so as to respond to it in that way. This determinism can, I think, be expressed in the following way. In patriarchal society women are offered very few subject positions in comparison to men, who may be said to suffer from a surfeit of the same. As a result, women play a secondary role in patriarchal society; they are 'objects' against which men define themselves, at least in part, as subjects. One of the few subject positions that is open to women lies in the field of love: as Byron has noted, 'Man's love is of man's life a thing apart/'Tis women's whole existence'. Furthermore, sex for a woman has traditionally been the most traumatic and the most essential part of love, for it involves the surrendering of her virginity, with which, again traditionally, her worth as a woman has often been equated. Therefore feminist attacks on the presentation of sex without love, or sex where women are treated as objects, may perhaps be regarded, at least in part, as an unconscious attempt by feminists to preserve and defend one of the most important sites of subjectivity for women. If this is the case, then there is something profoundly conservative about feminist writing on pornography, for it is implicitly accepting that sex and love are privileged sites for female subjectivity, and the intensity of some feminist attacks on pornography could be said to reflect an unconscious acquiescence in patriarchy's distribution of subject positions. A shorthand way of expressing this is to say that feminism defends what it is allowed to defend. Thus, although feminism is much healthier and more active in its attacks on pornography than are those writers who choose to write from a historical point of view, it is important for feminism to take into account how its targets are historically determined if it is not to perpetuate, even by opposing, the subject positions patriarchy assigns to it. Perhaps the shock of feminism embracing pornography would create a greater potential for radical change than feminism's criticism of it.

A corollary of the argument that pornography objectifies women is that it 'subjectifies' men. Nothing, I would argue, could be further from the truth. If the claim that men suffer from a surfeit of subject positions can be accepted, then it would seem logical to assert that what they seek in pornography is not further subjectivity but, on the contrary, a release from it. In short, men seek to shed their identity in pornography to achieve a state of selflessness or 'objectification', and this is borne out, I think, by analyses of pornographic material which show that it is ultimately concerned with phantasy. Take, for example, the 'come' shot when a woman swallows the semen that a man ejaculates over her face and breasts. A feminist interpretation of this might be that it shows the subordination of a woman to a man's pleasure, thereby presenting him in a dominant role. However, if, as I argue in my essay, pornography in part involves a realisation of the incestuous phantasy, then the 'come' shot takes on a very different meaning. For what the man does in ejaculating over the woman is in a sense to replicate the role of the mother giving milk to the infant. This gives a new understanding to the notion of the incestuous phantasy, for it is not, in the crude formulation, a little boy making love to his mother; rather it is the little boy *becoming* his mother. If this analysis is accepted, then pornography does not show, as some feminists have claimed, a hatred of women but rather a desire to become, at least in one respect, like them.

What the foregoing shows, I hope, is that there is still plenty to be said on the subject of pornography and sexual representation in general. What I have tried to do in this introduction is not to look at the various ways in which these topics can be studied – for example, through their effects – but to try and see what patterns lie behind the male and female contributors' respective views of pornography and then endeavour to show the implications of those patterns. The historical view functions to distance the men from the problem, while the women, although they realise the importance of the need to understand and act in the present, may be in danger of not seeing how history is making them collude with patriarchy. Another pattern that emerges from the women's contributions is that female sexuality is either objectified or in excess of the current regime of representations. This is, perhaps, the point where some connections can be made between the contributors, for Clive Bloom's piece on mechanisation can be assimilated to the process of objectification criticised by Alison Assiter in her article on popular fiction, while Mike Woolf's comments on the inability of ideology to accommodate and contain sexual desire find an echo in Laura Claridge's piece on Pope. These are signs that a dialogue has begun. It is up to the reader to continue it.

Part One
Historical

2

Grinding with the Bachelors
Pornography in a Machine Age

CLIVE BLOOM

The (dis)contents of a report: the *Final Report* of the Attorney General's Commission on Pornography, published July 1986, contained over 1000 pages in two volumes; the Commission had eleven sitting members, and drew on a range of local and federal reporting agencies, covering the whole United States, plus numerous highly qualified witnesses. This is the concern over pornography today in the most advanced technological nation in the world.[1]

A sense of helplessness pervades the Commission's findings. 'Ideally', one Commissioner writes,

> I would have preferred that our condemnation of materials directly affecting behavior be couched in more forceful language, and that our recommendations for enhanced law enforcement, particularly with respect to violent and degrading materials, be likewise more pronounced. The reluctance of some Commissioners to adopt more potent language . . . was undoubtedly attributable to the scarcity of definitive research on negative effects . . . more corroborative research may warrant firmer control measures.   (p. 27)

There is a faltering at the start, for there is no accurate measure of pornographic excess and evidence is not available to give 'conclusive' (p. 307) proof of 'negative effects'. Commissioners show 'reluctance' to make definitive statements about pornography and where it is located (morally and psychically). Above all, here at the outset the moralists' position and ability to condemn is fatally undermined by their lack of 'potent language'. Against pornography there is only the (im)potent language of bureaucracy.

9

Moreover, the potency of science cannot come to the aid of a commission set up to safeguard democratic ethical processes. The bureaucratic machine breaks down – its site (that of the laboratory or experimental environment), its machinery (the ruler, the measure, the calculator, the computer) and its arbitrators (the scientists themselves) fail to advance the cause of morality, for 'from a purely social scientific perspective there is no cogent evidence [of] negative behavioral effect' (p. 28).

Nevertheless, and paradoxically, *'despite* [my emphasis] the absence of clinical evidence linking *Class III* materials [the most diverse pornography of a non-violent nature] to antisocial behavior', several correlational connections disturb the Commission (p. 28). Those responsible for Class III pornography are seen to harm 'the natural bond between sex and affection', have an adverse impact 'on the family concept' (p. 27) and desensitise men to the abuse of women (p. 28). Hence, 'moral' (p. 29) responsibility is finally what has to be adjudged, an attitude toward moral health – equilibrium on the scale of the purely human. However, to reach such a judgement it is necessary to suppress the subjective element, for 'each Commissioner's personal value assessment . . . encumbered objective analysis' (p. 27).

In this way the process of adjudication underwrites its own failure, unable as it is to manage a machinery that has to be worked by humanity on behalf of humanity. The machinery is set up by morality and gains moral value by evaluating human worth, but it can only function objectively in its task of safeguarding humanity, if geared without the specific morality (and therefore lack of 'objectivity') of its inventors. Consequently the process records without a witness. With the presence of a witness the process breaks down, for the gaze of the recorder instantly regears the recorded message. Double-bind of a pernicious kind: objectivity can only exist with an agent to receive the message, but the agent changes the message; machines talk to machines, the tools of the process and of a communication without a message. In this way pornography, exploitation and the pornographic denial of human worth are safeguarded and escape scrutiny whilst intensely under the scrutineer's gaze.

What the scrutineer wishes to protect is clear if the methodology is not:

Most importantly, although we [the Commissioners] have

emphasized in our discussion of harms the kinds of harms that can most easily be observed and measured, the idea of harm is broader than that. To a number of us, the most important harms must be seen in moral terms, and the act of moral condemnation of that which is immoral is not merely important but essential. From this perspective there are acts that need be seen not only as causes of immorality but as manifestations of it. Issues of human dignity and human decency, no less real for their lack of scientific measurability, are for many of us central to thinking about the question of harm. And when we think about harm in this way, there are acts that must be condemned not because the evils of the world will thereby be eliminated, but because conscience demands it.   (p. 303)

The issue is plainly a moral one. Pornography poses the dilemma of human values and of human dignity. The 'human' in an easily recognisable form begins to emerge in the document from Washington.

Here is a clearly stated position against that which denies human worth and repels decent people – a consensus opinion informed by science to aid commonsense. Upheld are the virtues of the individual, the innocent (children), the unprotected (women), the domestic (home values and the family) and the state (the social orientation of the former categories). Against this there persists a barrage of low- and high-level obscenity:

Most American citizens have no idea that such gruesome scenes are common in the world of obscene publications today. When asked to describe what is currently on the market, they think in terms of airbrushed centrefolds in the popular 'men's magazines'. But steady customers of pornography have long since grown tired of simple heterosexual nudity. Indeed, a visit to an adult bookstore quickly reveals the absence of so-called 'normal' sexuality. The offerings today feature beribboned 18 to 20 year old women whose genitalia have been shaved to make them look like little girls and men giving enemas or whippings to one another and metal bars to hold a woman's legs apart and 3 foot rubber penises and photographs of women sipping ejaculate from champagne glasses. In one shop . . . there were 46 films for sale which depicted women having intercourse or performing

oral sex with . . . pigs, dogs, donkeys and horses. This is the
world of pornography today.   (pp. 74–5)

It is necessary to be definite. This is both appalling and frightening
because it is terrorism on the grandest scale and most dreadful
levels. The Commission cannot contemplate it and retreats in fear
and loathing.

Pornography becomes *the absolute* against which we measure our
own human dignity, our very sanity. Yet here it is at every level,
pervasive, sickly, fascinating and powerful, organised by groups
who themselves are masters of market research (organised crime) –
a major industry dealing in the technologies of film, publishing,
printing and advertising, adept at developing new areas of the
perverse, and at researching new techniques of retail exploitation
and of distribution: capitalism against itself.

At this point we are returned to the issue of potency: the state
defines itself as guardian of civil liberty, protector of civil rights,
yet all around this is abused through sexual exploitation on a
massive and an unprecedented scale. An invisible machinery works
an empire of signs of defeat for the state. What action can the state
take? Pornography appears endemic in Western democracy. Yet
to defend the democratic ideal the state needs to act. How does it
do so? By organising a commission.

The problem is indisputable even though the evidence is lacking:
'we, the people' feel the problem to be overwhelming – a veritable
plague. While evidence abounds on the streets, in cinemas, on
television, in libraries, this evidence remains the painfully visible
sign of impotence. Against whom does the State act: the consumers
or producers of pornography? A cleft stick.

The state must act against pornography and sexual obscenity in
the arts and media, yet, as has been said, its machinery works
against its requirements, rendering the visible (we see pornography
everywhere) invisible (the statistics fail to record it). In order to
act, the state must in effect cease to act, rigidify itself, pull in its
horns, activate its protective shell – customs officials, FBI, local
police, *agents provocateurs*. To fight terror against the individual,
the child, the woman and the family, all these must invoke terror –
the state invokes terror in the form of penal recrimination and
corporal punishments. In this instance the law collapses. Here is
the imitation of the non-logical on the state's behalf. How does it
work? With ironic fervour. Pornography is unquantifiable, the

forms it takes indefinable and multiple; the pornographer is usually invisible, the harm pornography does is alarmingly impossible to gauge. To fight this the state calls for harsher penalties, greater sanctions: its actions therefore fail to follow its words. To fight the invisible we invoke the absurd and do nothing, for in this instance pornography is itself nothing.

So far I have traced the work of pornography in its relationship with the people and the state. In this model, which works today in advanced societies, the measures of the people and the state, taken in aggregate, amount to a failure of nerves and conscience when faced with the absurd. Pornography in attacking human dignity also attacks the essence of human nature. To do this pornography itself must become an essence acting ahistorically on the 'core' of an unchanged human experience of the quality of life.

Only within this framework can we trace the pornographer's activity and effects. But this must defeat us. Another place, perhaps invisible to us, now must be sought. In the following pages such a place will be sought and another definition of pornography will be offered. We must seek evidence that perhaps betrays a motive unsought by the well intentioned and rightly indignant members of the Attorney General's Commission.

Pornography is not an essence but a social construct that manipulates and positions its viewers and readers within historical time. While it plays with biological conditions it nevertheless historicises them and puts them into a recognisable social framework. The biological givens and the numerous (yet finite) positions they offer are eroticised *into* history by the artist and eroticist/pornographer (I make no distinction as yet). By this I mean that each age has its choice position, its detailed anatomical point of desire (the late twentieth century chooses breast and buttock, mouth and anus, for instance). These points of desire (reducible each to its 'other') change rapidly from age to age (hands and ankles, skin itself and buttocks in the nineteenth century; legs in the 1930s and 1940s; waists and busts in the 1950s). Indeed, positions and activities correspond to both place and time (whipping and spanking as the English perversions).

All this shows clearly that specificity is needed in our attempts to understand the pornographic. Moreover, pornography supports both male (including homosexual) and female self-understandings.

Hence 'masculinity' – a masculinity itself constructed within history and without essence – may be the most dreadful ideological construct to support pornography, but not the only one. Feminism, itself a construct to cope with oppression, does not yet deal with this problem in an adequate way: as a symptomatic *response* it is always and only *just that* – caught within an ideological, cultural (therefore *historical*) moment. Furthermore, the emergent gay movements liberate alongside themselves a pornographic double that feeds their membership's needs and which uses the same iconography as heterosexual erotica.

If I pause here it is only because so much in the volumes on erotica in our libraries tells us so little – so much description, so little history. Where then shall a beginning be made? Not in ancient times, for that would reawaken the old invitation to ahistoricism. Instead, let us choose a moment, itself vague, yet more modern at least. Let us choose 1829 as our point of departure for this inquiry. It must be noted that this is a point of convenience and not an absolute, a point where a mythology for its age appears embodied in Thomas Carlyle's 'Signs of the Times'.[2]

Carlyle was the most eloquent of the recorders of change and, reading back into the latter half of the previous century, he comments,

> How often have we heard, for the last fifty years, that the country was wrecked, and fast sinking; whereas, up to this date, the country is entire and afloat! The 'State in Danger' is a condition of things, which we have witnessed a hundred times; and as for the Church, it has seldom been out of 'danger' since we can remember it.[3]

Nevertheless, a crisis, a profound change has occurred and Carlyle attempts to delineate it and its power:

> Were we required to characterize this age of ours by any single epithet, we should be tempted to call it, not an Heroical, Devotional, Philosophical, or Moral Age, but, above all others the Mechanical Age. It is the Age of Machinery. . . . Our old modes of exertion are all discredited, and thrown aside. On every hand, the living artisan is driving from his workshop, to make room for a speedier, inanimate one.[4]

As with industry, so with the state and the apparatus of civilised activity among men:

> Has any man, or any society of men, a truth to speak, a piece of spiritual work to do; they can nowise proceed at once and with the natural organs, but must first call a public meeting, appoint committees. . . . With individuals, in like manner, natural strength avails little. No individual now hopes to accomplish the poorest enterprise single-handed and without mechanical aids; he must make interest with some existing corporation. . . . Philosophy, Science, Act, Literature, all depend on machinery . . . so that books are not only printed, but, in a great measure, written and sold, by machinery.[5]

Carlyle here presents a paradigm of the rise of state bureaucracy and corporate man. The modern world has begun: machine capitalism supported by state bureaucracy. This is farsighted of Carlyle, for this new age had hardly commenced and the new situation had not fully materialised in the 1820s. It points us forward to another age. Yet it goes some way towards explaining the dilemma of the Washington Commission sitting horrified and dismayed through 1986. Here again is Carlyle:

> To us who live in the midst of all this, and see continually the . . . practice of every one founded on Mechanism . . . it is apt to seem quite natural, and as if it could never have been otherwise. . . . The domain of Mechanism . . . can at any time embrace but a limited portion of man's interests. . . . .
>
> To speak a little pedantically, there is a science of *Dynamics* in man's fortunes and nature, as well as of *Mechanics*. There is a science which treats of, and practically addresses, the primary, unmodified forces and energies of man, the mysterious springs of Love, and Fear, and Wonder, of Enthusiasm, Poetry, Religion, all which have a true vital and *infinite* character.[6]

1829–1986: a continuity and again a double-bind. Our Commissioners, knowing that this has not always been the way it was (pornography as epidemic), knowing that such a view of the situation does not make it 'quite natural' and that 'things have been otherwise', nevertheless invoke a 'science' of 'mechanics' in order to defend a model based on Carlylean '*Dynamics*' and on the notion of essence, 'on the mind which is within us' and 'the primary . . . energies of man'.[7] Failing to grasp historical process, the Commission, like Carlyle, invokes a mythic model of human activity and interaction. The Commissioners find themselves in a historical timewarp, acting as the 'new' Carlylean bureaucrats of the early nineteenth century, defenders of industrial capitalism, moralists betrayed by good intentions into a modern 'reaction' to the Machine Age. Carlyle's paradigm is theirs too. Carlyle is our starting-point because he helped define the 'modern' as the already *outdated* – the logic of profit and of the prophet.

Paralleling the rise of industry and bureaucracy from the late eighteenth century, the Gothic experience in art allowed for the release of perverse pastoral instincts and the expression of an erotics suppressed by historical and realistic novels. Politically authoritarian and conservative in nature, yet able to act as an outlet for sexually repressed sensibilities, the Gothic was at once a release and a suppression (a representation of and reduction of human experience to the absurd, illegal, violent, deadly, erotic and irrational). It dealt in the logistics of hidden power and it arose alongside its twin, the Romantic novel.

Within the Gothic comes a relatively new attitude – indissolubly linked are death and eros. The dead become objects not of fear but of desire, in a secret restless desire for the forbidden. This 'new' eroticism appears in de Sade, Maturin, Keats, Poe, Baudelaire and many others. The erotic form can be either male or female or a perfect combination. The world of visual art took up the cause: 'the works of Fuseli and Etty are only a few examples . . . of the emotions aroused by the dead body and the beautiful victim. In the world of the imagination, death and violence have merged with desire. . . . Intercourse with the dead occurs frequently in the works of Sade.'[8]

The Gothic extols the virtues of the body as object, the beautiful moment as the embodiment of passivity and availability. There is no holding back – no coming to life at the last minute: death *is* the erotic as bodies are offered gift-wrapped and boxed for their unknown lovers to open and penetrate. Here, then, on the verge of the Industrial Revolution the erotic has altered its course; the 'new' eroticism involves the invitation of passivity and the seduction of the living by the blandishments of the bodily orifices of the dead. The victim (the corpse) becomes morally culpable by his or her very presence, and the aggressor (the pornographer) becomes the dead seducer's last victim! Throughout the late eighteenth and the whole of the nineteenth century, living and breathing mortals affected the seductive pose of the dead making a virtue out of illness – making disease erotic:

> For snobs and parvenus and social climbers, TB was one index of being genteel, delicate, sensitive. With the new mobility (social and geographical) made possible in the eighteenth century, worth and station are not given; they must be asserted. They were asserted through new notions about clothes ('fashion') and new attitudes toward illness. Both clothes (the outer garment of the body) and illness (a kind of interior decor of the body) became tropes for new attitudes toward the self. . . .
> Consumption was understood as a manner of appearing, and that appearance became a staple of nineteenth-century manners. . . . It was glamorous to look sickly. . . . The TB-influenced idea of the body was a new model for aristocratic looks – at a moment when aristocracy stops being a matter of power, and starts being mainly a matter of image.[9]

Consumption – a disease for industrial (i.e. consumer) society. Kafka's 'A Hunger Artist' clearly connects this image to the early twentieth century. Consumption was an aristocratic ideal placed in reach of the displaced *moral* aristocrat – the Romantic artist.

In 1855–6, at the height of Britain's industrial might, Henry Wallis painted *Chatterton*, a picture mythologising the artistic rebel, dying in his garret and destroyed by the world of the philistine. Chatterton's death is presented for the consumption of the very bourgeoisie who 'killed' him. His androgynous body, pale (consumptive) and marble-white, lies on a bed while through the open window an escape route is offered for the artistic essence (for the soul is *not* present). His hair is a passionate red though his body is pale and dead. *Chatterton* (painted in *chemical* pigments) overtly denies the effects of the Industrial Revolution (technology) as it celebrates the artist (nature, the essence of the human). Yet, in inverse proportion it celebrates the opposite of this, for new artists *have to die* to have power, and their bodies, which are consumed by a willing public who flock to the gallery, have to be prone, passive, eroticised by death (the 'femininity' of his attitude suggests

a parody of the couched nude, the post-orgasmic houri). We enter
(as viewers) a chamber reminiscent of a Gothic cave where a partly
dressed androgyne lays waiting for the penetration of our gaze.
He lies there for our gaze; his purpose is to lie there in order to
confirm his power as an artist and our power as philistines over
him – irony of art. *Chatterton*, as a picture, confirms the power of
the Machine Age and the power of the machine gaze.

On all levels, the overt and the covert, this celebration of the
machinic continued into the twentieth century. Throughout the
previous century the pale, tuberculous body and the marble dead
are matched in their alienated half-life by the automaton and the
doll: E. T. A. Hoffman's 'doll' and Shelley's Frankenstein monster
are followed by similar figures in Poe ('The Facts in the Case of M.
Valdemar') and Melville ('The Bell Tower'). By the twentieth
century the automaton has become man's 'other': the robot.

The representation of the robotic and alienated machine slave
coincides with the rise of production-line industrial processes. Art
is not free from this, for modernism happily celebrating the
'modern' is cognisant of the social realm and its new dynamism.
Most major artists followed this movement, reflecting it in their
work. For example, T. S. Eliot (a private and public pornographer,
who would, so Virginia Woolf reports, put on green make-up and
pretend to be deathly ill and who also took a special interest in
murders) takes up the 'modern' in his early poetry. Kafka reflects
the age too, as does Marcel Duchamp (in the glass construction,
The Bride Stripped Bare by her Bachelors, Even). Reactions against the
'modern' merely reflect its power. Reactions in favour of the
'modern' run into the popular genre of science fiction and the
high-art movement of Futurism. Futurist manifestos declared
that the modern and the technological had arrived as suitable
replacements for the outmoded and the pre-industrial.

Hence, 'the Futurists saw the practice of art as a form of energy
capable of playing a role in the management of civil affairs, to such
an extent that no productive element . . . should remain untouched
by it'.[10] Moreover, 'it is undeniable that the authors [of their
manifestos] foresaw the possibility of substituting mechanical
devices in the performance of functions which were then still held
to be the sole perogative of human beings'.[11] They declared that
'there is no essential difference between a human brain and a

machine' and that 'poetry must consist of straight lines and calculus'.[12] Both Walt Whitman with his celebration of the modern in *Leaves of Grass* and Maxime du Camp with *Les Chants modernes* (1855) were popular with the Futurists. The Futurists' ideal of putting 'the spectator in the centre of the picture' coincided with the creation of a 'hymn [to] the man at the wheel'.[13]

While the Futurists spoke of and attempted to come to terms with the energy and rhythm of modern industrialised man, other artists saw clearly that the eroticism that arose out of such a vision could lead to an erotics of the human 'other' – the doll. Hans Bellmer's dolls are dead, passive, seductive. They exist as bit-parts which eroticise the whole body as if the body simply consisted of interchangeable parts (see, for example, *La Poupée* and *The Machine-Gunneress*). Bellmer's dolls exist in a continual slippage of meaning: hairless and infantilised, the dolls are machined, cold and contorted, exposing an anus as if it were a mouth, an armpit as if it were a vagina. The vulnerability of these dolls is their very strength, for the totally eroticised body is anathema – a horror which fascinates and repels. These dolls conjure up not Oedipal nightmares but Machine Age nightmares – availability without response – a masturbatory and alienating pleasure which coincides with fear of the perfect and the absurd and the absolute.

Henry Wallis's picture of Chatterton, which covertly celebrates machine power, finds its echo in the Futurists' overt desire to celebrate that some power (both used photographs and photographic techniques). I have suggested that the Surrealist Bellmer completes the movement I have traced with his exposition of woman as machine automaton – an erotics of petrified and processed objects.

The previous sections of this essay have attempted to trace two cultural movements. The first is the dual rise of a corporate and technologised humanity while the second is the celebration and reflection of that humanity in the distorted mirror of art (at least, certain modes of 'artistic' expression). One of the features of this expression is the combining of eroticism and dead passivity culminating in the celebration of an erotics of the dead as automatons and machines. Here the priorities are reversed, for an erotics of the machine now appears to predate an erotics of the body. The struggles of the Commission on Pornography can be seen to be already underwritten by a self-defeating principle – that is, human dignity – for the machinic (the scientific laboratory, the behavioural process, the statistic) is the *only* method of prioritising the body (human dignity) once more. Consequently, human dignity (our essential nature) is *guaranteed* by our equivalence to machines capable of measurement and available for measurement. As already shown, the Commission was defeated *because* of the very presence of scientists and administrators who brought the quantifiably problematic to their work – namely, human value systems. This is where the pornographic creeps stealthily back into the system which had been designed to identify and eradicate it. Too many people concerned with the problem of pornography, while they understand it is about power, think that that power is underwritten by sexuality. Pornography knows that sexuality is only its expression. The laws governing it (in this writer's opinion) are otherwise.

How is this so? Quite evidently pornography deals in sexuality. Here real people *are* exploited: women, children, adolescents. Where pornography breaks off from eroticism is in its non-mutual exploitative attitude to that which it displays. The pornographic appetite is therefore a degraded anti-human appetite. Whoever is the pornographic 'victim' displayed in films, books or magazines (and it need not always be women, for pornography exploits for a market and the market evolves) is constantly reduced to the condition of a mere orifice. Hence, in pornography, with its emphasis on anatomical detail, the *who* is always translated into the *what*: this *what* embraces not merely the actions in pornography but also the actors.

Combined with this is a denial of the role of the central tenet of individuality in the last 200 years (at least from 1780): that is, the notion of imaginative involvement in fantasy by the viewer/reader. Pornography *states* its subject matter in order to *deny* imagination (unlike, in the final analysis, Bellmer's work, which is 'art'). The beholder does not imagine himself within the pornographic activity of the picture. This may seem strange, but the contention is straightforward: denial of the imaginative processes is central to power structures geared to deny individuality and intervention.

Hence pornography's obscene nature, for pornographic material excludes the viewer; his powerlessness is reflected in his erection, which can only be relieved by 'self-application'. Pornography involves narcissism *because* it denies access to those in the picture or book. The pornographic appetite is therefore reclusive and autistic, given to people whose personality has been wholly or partly denied access to societal interaction; pornography is the province of the cut-off, lonely and ashamed in society (who may be any 'respectable' person).

The narcissism pornography induces is the belief in the power of one's sexuality at the point where that is rendered impotent by society. The pornographic appetite is therefore enraged against society (it is thrown into the 'I'll teach society a lesson' syndrome). Because women are so frequently offered up as *unavailable* in pornography it induces a rage against women as representatives of society's power. What pornography gives access to is the self, but a perverse 'self' generated by exclusion and impotence. That is why pornography caters for the same basic drives as body-building magazines, survivalist magazines and 'true detective' magazines, for all of these deal in a narcissistic substitute for really effective and socially interactive power-sharing. It is no coincidence that the Commission on Pornography reprints an article on the relationship between 'true detective' magazines and sex offences by some of the purchasers of those magazines (pp. 55–69).

At this point it may be useful to retrace my argument and pull some of the threads together. I have been concerned to show that from the early Industrial Revolution to the present a movement of depersonalisation has taken place such that man sees himself in aggregate and as an individual in terms of machine technology. Consequent upon this first movement, which is well documented in contemporary writings, is a second, less well-noticed movement in the erotic arts which celebrate in perverse fashion that first alienating experience. This second movement came to terms with the first by depicting it through the representation of death and a death-in-life disease.

The *Final Report* of the Attorney General's Commission is a consequence of these two movements and a product of them. In attempting to defend human dignity and the human essence, the very tools of analysis deny (through their machine accuracy) the human agents wielding them. The Commissioners are defeated because the committee system (as Carlyle pointed out) is a product of bureaucratic technology, and that technology (of expert opinion) cannot go beyond the concept of the human and analyse the motivating forces behind and working through the human. This committee is caught in its own history beyond which it cannot reach, for, by its very analytic processes, it shows its own ambivalence toward the subject it studies. Morality is underwritten by machine technology and the human essence becomes 'other' than itself while true to itself. Hence, the subjective (and therefore, the erotic) are one with the productive forces of the subjective: namely, the industrial. Consideration of human worth in these terms becomes meaningless, as Gilles Deleuze and Félix Guattari pointed out in 1972 in *Anti-Oedipus*. They tell us,

> We make no distinction between man and nature: the human essence of nature and the natural essence of man become one within nature in the form of production or industry. . . . Industry is then no longer considered from the extrinsic point of view of utility, but rather from the point of view of its fundamental identity with nature as production of man and by man.[14]

It is not my intention here to underwrite the need to put 'man' back into the productive system as an active agent, or to consider Deleuze and Guattari's own concerns with the 'subject' within the context of the anti-psychiatry movement. I do, however, wish to suggest that these two theorists of 'heroic' schizophrenia celebrate it in terms of the machine and its opposite, 'the body . . . as undifferentiated fluid'.[15] In this essay I have tried to show that these oppositions are, in truth, one and the same, and perform similar and complementary ideological functions.

In all this the bizarre may stand as confirmation of the normal. The most extreme form of masculine alienation in modern society is the psychopathic killer. Elsewhere I have documented the rise of the psychopath, which I date to the rise of technological specialisation in the late nineteenth century.[16] At this point the technological expertise of the forces of order coincide with the powerful urges and expressive actions of psychopathic delirium. I argued that psychopathic action is caused not by unconscious urges but by a will both controlled (by the individual) and (socially) out of control. Jack the Ripper was the mirror-image of his forensic pursuers.

During the late twentieth century the same phenomenon can be observed in the behaviour of two mass killers: Dennis Nilsen, who was arrested in February 1983 for the multiple murder of young men at his flats in North London, and Peter Sutcliffe, who murdered or attacked twenty women between July 1975 and January 1981 in Yorkshire and whom the press dubbed 'the Yorkshire Ripper'.[17]

Although neither man was motivated by pornography to kill, they represent the extreme end of the spectrum of alienation I have described. Both Nilsen and Sutcliffe came from deeply disturbed families (in her psychotic delirium Sutcliffe's wife thought he was an 'aeroplane'). From these beginnings both developed considerably perverse attitudes to the dead. Sutcliffe was a gravedigger who enjoyed 'playing' with corpses and who eventually heard apocalyptic voices while standing in a grave, and Nilsen enjoyed the image of his own 'dead' body reflected back by mirrors. He also casually dissected and drew his victims' bodies. Both Sutcliffe and Nilsen developed their bodies – an autistic occupation which 'entails no relation to others'.[18] Moreover, both men were 'misfits' who could not fit in with modern life (industrial for Sutcliffe and bureaucratic for Nilsen) and who felt themselves 'artistic' and 'intellectual'. Sutcliffe said that when he murdered he was 'doing his job' – a perverse justification of the killing of women who walked out at night (not always prostitutes). Noticeably, both men were geared toward machines – Sutcliffe toward motorbike engines and cars and Nilsen toward his music, which he listened to on headphones and after which he killed.

This grisly catalogue of machine alienation may be extended by the reader who follows up the documentation of these cases. It can be summarised, at least for Peter Sutcliffe, as follows:

Sutcliffe's attempt to descend upon Sheffield, move as it were from the places of the first Industrial Revolution to the second, makes sense in this perspective. You could also say it was inevitable, because of his fascination with motors. A whole series of heroic models combine Man with the Motor to produce Superman. The term, 'Bachelor Machines' has even been coined. . . . 'Bachelor' because man, ignoring woman, mates with the machine. Many such machines (as in Kafka, Jarry, Roussel) are torture machines; others are masturbatory. They have haunted the nineteenth and twentieth century imagination, from Poe to the Dadaists and the Surrealists. They represent machines as 'male' – excluding female – and an imaginary attempt to gain mastery, by harnessing the machine and making it take the place of all that is 'other' (in eroticism, in religion, in power-structures). . . .

It has been remarked earlier that Sutcliffe uses his bullworker and his motors to construct an artificial masculinity.

The tools he uses for killing are also sexual and industrial.[19]

Death, passivity, machines, eroticism: the body is newly eroticised as it becomes machinic; the machinic becomes erotic as it becomes human. Man, left human and 'other' by his machines and by his need for the erotic, is forced into pornography by his exclusion from the sources of the power he seeks – the power of the erotic and of the machine. Pornography's sleight of hand allows us the illusion of power as it fantasises away that power, as it makes totally open and avoidable the very objects we may never possess, as it tricks us with our own essence.

The Bachelors grind their own chocolate – *perpetuum mobile*.[20]

NOTES

1. Attorney General's Commission on Pornography, *Final Report* (Washington, DC: US Department of Justice, 1986) vol. 1. All page references in text.
2. Thomas Carlyle, 'Signs of the Times', in *The Victorian Prophets*, ed. Peter Keating (London: Fontana, 1981) pp. 44–68.
3. Ibid., p. 45.
4. Ibid., p. 47.
5. Ibid., pp. 48–9.
6. Ibid., p. 55.
7. Ibid., p. 54.
8. Philippe Ariès, *The Hour of our Death*, tr. Helen Weaver (Harmondsworth: Peregrine, 1983) pp. 375–6.
9. Susan Sontag, *Illness as Metaphor* (Harmondsworth: Penguin, 1983) pp. 32–3.
10. Umbro Apollonio (ed.), *Futurist Manifestos*, tr. Robert Brain, R. W. Flint, J. C. Higgitt and Caroline Tisdall (London: Thames and Hudson, 1973) p. 7.
11. Ibid., p. 9.
12. Ibid., pp. 8 and 15.
13. Ibid., pp. 16 and 21.
14. Gilles Deleuze and Félix Guattari, *Anti-Oedipus*, tr. Robert Hurley, Mark Seem and Helen R. Lane (New York: Viking Press, 1977) p. 4.
15. Ibid., pp. 1 and 9.

16. See Clive Bloom, 'The House that Jack Built: Jack the Ripper, Legend and the Power of the Unknown', in Clive Bloom, Brian Docherty, Jane Gibb and Keith Shand (eds), *Nineteenth-Century Suspense* (London: Macmillan, 1988) pp. 120–37.
17. All information from Nicole Ward Jouve, *'The Street-Cleaner': The Yorkshire Ripper Case on Trial* (London: Marion Boyars, 1986); and Brian Masters, *Killing for Company* (London: Coronet, 1985).
18. Jouve, *'The Street Cleaner'*, p. 71.
19. Ibid., pp. 156 and 158.
20. The Bachelors who 'grind their own chocolate' appear in Marcel Duchamp's *Large Glass* (*The Bride Stripped Bare by her Bachelors, Even*). The phrase refers to a little-used slang euphemism for masturbation which can be found slightly altered to grinding 'coffee' in D. H. Lawrence, *Lady Chatterley's Lover* (Ch. 14).

3

Disseminating Desire
Grove Press and 'The End[s] of Obscenity'

RICHARD ELLIS

The End of Obscenity[1] is the title of a book published in the late 1960s written by Charles Rembar. It details the processes by which it became possible in the United States at the beginning of that decade to publish books which had been previously held to be unpublishable for fear of prosecution on the grounds of obscenity. Rembar seeks to define the processes by which the US courts in the late fifties and early sixties came to adopt what he sees as a markedly changed attitude to censorship, an assumption best encapsulated by Norman Mailer's bold assertion in the book's Foreword that 'A war has been won' (*EO*, p. x). In this period, certainly, there was a clear increase in the number of obscenity cases brought to the courts, as made apparent by P. R. MacMillan in his detailed exploration, *Censorship and Public Morality*.[2] MacMillan in his book makes frequent reference to Norman St John Stevas's *Obscenity and the Law*, published in 1956.[3] These three books, taken together, provide three contrasting but compatible perspectives on this 'war': Stevas provides an antedated, preparatory critique of the history and philosophy of legal censorship; Rembar offers the reader exciting accounts of the cut and thrust of some of the courtroom battles of this period; and MacMillan a more distanced analysis invoking precedent and statute in detail.

The similarities between the three books are significant. First, we should note that all three were written by lawyers and take as their focus the interaction between obscenity and the law. Any discussion of obscenity in this period therefore needs to recognise that it must in some way be functioning on the cusp between, to employ Gramsci's terms, *dominazione* (domination) and *egemonia* (hegemony) in so far as (switching to Althusserian terminology, legitimately, since here his debt to Gramsci is direct) law and the

26

legal system can be regarded as both an Ideological and a Repressive State Apparatus.[4] If an end to obscenity can in any sense be detected, then some sort of (ideological) repositioning of pornography within the social formation is occurring. The second point I wish to stress initially is that these three books constantly remind us that censorship confrontations in the United Kingdom and the United States are publishers' and booksellers' battles (rather than authors') and that characteristically, in the period under scrutiny, publishers were the main courtroom protagonists.

Rembar's account makes this plain. His book possesses a very clear chronological span: the seven-year period from 1959 and the US trials of *Lady Chatterley's Lover* (in New York City's Post Office Department and subsequently in the Supreme Court) through to the Brennan Supreme Court opinion of 21 March 1966 and its immediate aftermath: the publication of *Last Exit to Brooklyn* and *The Story of O*. The cases Rembar closely examines are those in which he was involved as an attorney, and during this period he acted for Grove Press, the publisher of *Lady Chatterley's Lover, Tropic of Cancer, Last Exit to Brooklyn, The Story of O* and *The Naked Lunch*.[5]

Rembar traces in narrative form the step-by-step processes by which the US Courts came first to admit 'prurience' as not broadly appealing to 'lustful thoughts', but more restrictedly, as appealing to 'shameful or morbid interest' (*EO*, p. 141), and secondly to allow as admissible evidence 'redeeming social importance' and, later, 'redeeming social value' (*EO*, p. 489). For Rembar, each of these revisions of the discourse of censorship marks an erosion of the legal applicability of the concept of obscenity. But, as his story unfolds, it becomes apparent that Rembar's own sympathies alter: unhesitatingly in favour of the unrestricted publication of *Lady Chatterley* in 1959, he cannot so confidently endorse publications released after the successful defence in 1966 of John Cleland's *Memoirs of a Woman of Pleasure* (usually known as *Fanny Hill*)[6] had established so completely the 'utterly without redeeming social value' formula: 'The current uses of the new freedom are not all to the good . . . [with their] present distorted, impoverished, masturbatory concentration on representations of sex' (*EO*, pp. 489–92).

This sense of unease was widespread, and *The Naked Lunch* in particular frequently proved to be the stumbling-block. A judge's censorship-trial summing-up printed in *Evergreen Review* in 1965 might be regarded as symptomatic:

It appears to me abundantly clear that the book, in almost every part, goes substantially past the customary limits of candor . . . and that applying contemporary standards its appeal taken as a whole is to prurient interest, that is to . . . shameful or morbid interest. I cannot say that its predominant appeal is such or that it is matter utterly without redeeming social importance, taken as a whole. It appears to me, therefore, and I find that the material is not obscene . . . .[7]

The problems posed by *The Naked Lunch* as a narrative should be explanation enough of this judge's unease and confusion. Passages such as the following are difficult for many readers to come to terms with:

Mark and Mary are suddenly impatient and hot. . . . They push Johnny forward onto the gallows platform covered with moldy jockstraps and sweat shirts. Mark is adjusting the noose.

'Well, here you go.' Mark starts to push Johnny off the platform.

Mary: 'No, let me.' She locks her hands behind Johnny's buttocks, puts her forehead against him, smiling into his eyes she moves back, pulling him off the platform into space. . . . His face swells with blood. . . . Mark reaches up with one lithe movement and snaps Johnny's neck . . . sound like a stick broken in wet towels. A shudder runs down Johnny's body . . . one foot flutters like a trapped bird. . . . Mark has draped himself over a swing and mimics Johnny's twitches, closes his eyes and sticks his tongue out. . . . Johnny's cock springs up and Mary guides it up her cunt, writhing against him in a fluid belly dance, groaning and shrieking with delight . . . sweat pours down her body, hair hangs over her face in wet strands. 'Cut him down, Mark,' she screams. Mark reaches over with a snap knife and cuts the rope, catching Johnny as he falls, easing him onto his back with Mary still impaled and writhing. . . . She bites away Johnny's lips and nose and sucks out his eyes with a pop. . . . She tears off great hunks of cheek. . . . Now she lunches on his prick. . . . Mark walks over to her and she looks up from Johnny's half-eaten genitals, her face covered with blood, eyes phosphorescent. . . . Mark puts his foot on her shoulder and kicks her over on her back. . . . he leaps on her, fucking her insanely . . . they roll from one end of the room to the other, pinwheel end-over-end and leap high in the air like great hooked fish.[8]

Obviously this extract from the section 'A. J.'s Annual Party' has to be relocated within its narrative frame: the protagonists are placed at the start of this section on a raised stage; they will end up looked 'tired and petulant, like actors in a blue movie'; and the section as a whole is one more mind-projection of the overall, but mostly invisible narrator, William Lee. This junkie protagonist, fleeing because 'the heat is on', encounters on the subway an 'exec-type fruit', satirically offers him an anecdote featuring 'straight' caricatures of the inhabitants of the drug underground, thereby playing upon the executive's prejudices, and then in turn explores/exploits these media clichés himself in the book's central sections in a collage-like (pre-cut-up) exploration of the 'face of total need' experienced at the drug-addicted base of the capitalist power-pyramid set up by 'the algebra of need'.[9] What is offered in this complex, reflexively ludic narrative structure is, in the phrase of one of the best critics of Burroughs, a 'science of dreams'.[10] In the continuing desire of censors to examine such passages as this in isolation, however, we have to recognise a broader-based communal unease; as Rembar tersely puts it, 'It cannot be stressed too often it was the United States Constitution that saved these books, and not the will of the people' (*EO*, p. 174). One cannot here avoid the wry observation that, forced to abandon 'the will of the people' as justification for his advocacy, Rembar resorts to the US Constitution; but, more importantly, we can now begin to locate the obvious discursive fissures in both the ambivalent opinion of the judge and the narrative of Rembar. It is surely appropriate to invoke Macherey's image of the pull of an 'absent sun' upon ideology, drawing their narratives at these points into a 'determinate disarray' in accord with a dominant social discourse seeking to conceal real contradictions in the social formation. We must, therefore, seek to account for the reasons why such 'unacceptable' texts were at this time published.[11]

Twice now in this discussion of the path traced by definitions of obscenity in the period 1959 to 1966 I have had cause to invoke the concept of ideology functioning through censorship's discourse, controlling social apprehensions of obscenity and the social role of censorship. Yet plainly what I have also portrayed is a seven-year period in which such an exacting narrative as *The Naked Lunch* could come to be published, along with other, long-banished texts such as *Lady Chatterley*, *Tropic of Cancer* and *Fanny Hill*. This fundamental assault on the term 'obscenity' in the dominant ideological discourse requires some sort of contextual explanation; and we must begin this process by restating that this victory was won not by writers but by publishers. On the face of it, their role would seem to have been at least libertarian. But it is difficult not to be pushed further than this, since censorship takes two main forms – repression of the obscene and repression of political materials – and because this coincidence is frequently seen to be more causal than casual. As William Seagle expressed it, 'in the last analysis, all censorship is political censorship'.[12] The temptation must then be to see publishers involved in this conflict as not only libertarian but also politically radical in some way. I want, therefore, to begin my exploration of the contexts of the 'end of obscenity', by undermining such a deduction. I shall seek to do this by examining, as a necessary initial step, publishing's particular material situation in the late fifties, and shall take as my main focus Grove Press, the publishing house most centrally involved in these censorship controversies.

A starting-point would be to take up Thomas Whiteside's contention in his *Blockbuster Complex*[13] that 'Drastic Changes' have occurred in the publishing industry since 'the early nineteen-sixties' (*BC*, p. 1). 'Drastic Changes' is in fact the title of his first chapter, and the changes in question are usually attributed by commentators to a process of conglomeration – eloquently described by Whiteside at the start of his book:

> In the past twenty years or so, the hardcover trade-book houses of Alfred A. Knopf and Pantheon Books were taken over by Random House, and Random House was acquired by RCA. Random House then acquired the formerly independent paper-back publishing company Ballantine Books. And then RCA sold Random House to Newhouse Publications, which owns the Newhouse newspaper chain. In the last four years, Dell Publishing, one of the principal mass-market paperback houses, was acquired by Doubleday & Company, the largest trade book publisher in the country, which had previously acquired, among other enterprises, the Literary Guild, the nation's second-largest

book club. Another mass-market-paperback house, Fawcett Publication, was acquired by CBS, which had already acquired yet
another mass-market-paperback house, Popular Library, and the
hardcover house Holt, Rinehart & Winston. The hardcover house
Bobbs-Merrill was acquired by the International Telephone &
Telegraph Corporation. Pocket Books, a leading paperback publisher, was acquired, as part of the hardcover house Simon &
Schuster, by the conglomerate Gulf & Western, which also
owned Paramount Pictures. G. P. Putnam's Sons, which had
acquired the trade-book house of Coward, McCann & Geoghegan
and the paperback publisher Berkeley Books, was acquired by
MCA, which had earlier acquired Universal Pictures.

(*BC*, pp. 2–3)

This catalogue continues for another half-page before concluding,
'And this is only a partial listing of corporate mergers in the
publishing business in the recent past' (*BC*, p. 3).

Whiteside follows most commentators in locating the commence-
ment of this process in the sixties, in his case 1960 (*BC*, p. 3). I
want, however, to question this chronology. It seems to me
inadequate to regard the merger of Knopf and Random as a cause.
Instead, it is better seen as a symptom, and Whiteside's later
summary of the business histories of Knopf and Random supports
this contention:

one step . . . toward establishing the value of the Random House
estate [occurred] . . . in October of 1959 [when] thirty percent of
Cerf's and Klopfer's stock was offered for sale. . . .
    The stock market was booming, and before long several other
privately owned book-publishing companies followed the lead
of Random in putting substantial blocks of their stock up for
sale.   (*BC*, pp. 6–7)

Already, the key date has been silently pushed back into the fifties;
more crucially, what has now arisen, setting aside the particular
reason for the Random House decision, is the question of why
there was a movement in publishing away from private and
towards public ownership. Profits from a stock-market boom can
provide only a part of the answer; more usually, the move would
be seen as evidence of capitalisation requirements in an industry.
In the case of the publishing industry, there did indeed exist

definable capitalisation pressures which, I would contend, were coming to a head in the late 1950s. One needs to proceed cautiously here: obviously, for example, mass literacy had been an established feature of British and American mainstream culture for well over half a century. Similarly, advances in book-production techniques had made books an affordable commodity since the mid to late nineteenth century, and the publisher had for several decades longer assumed a recognisably contemporary guise: 'neither writer, nor printer, nor directly seller of [the] product but instead at the nodal point in the structure formed by the intersection of these three'.[14] Similarly, it might be said that the process of conglomeration had begun at least prior to the Second World War. Whiteside admits this (*BC*, p. 3). As Raymond Williams points out in *The Long Revolution*, 'ownership and control of the means of production has narrowed' throughout the twentieth century,[15] a process Charles Madison's book *Book Publishing in America* describes in detail.[16]

Even the much-vaunted paperback revolution was well advanced in the 1940s. Penguin Books, after all, had begun publishing in 1935, and its American imitator, Pocket Books, in 1939 (*BPA*, p. 546ff.). Indeed, it can be claimed that it was the reading requirements of soldiers during the Second World War that really established the paperback reading habit.[17] Madison defines this process:

> The war effort in the early 1940s greatly stimulated the expansion of paperback publishing [via] the Council on Books in Wartime, founded in 1942 . . . [which] concentrated on supplying readable books to the armed forces. . . . In all, 123,535,305 copies of Armed Services Editions were printed during the war . . . [and] greatly stimulated paperback publishing.   (*BPA*, p. 548)

This trend continued into the fifties: 'paperback sales rose fast . . . [and] At that time there developed first in the USA the so-called "Egg Head" paperbacks'.[18] Grove Press brought out its first quality 'Evergreen Books' paperback in 1954 (*BPA*, p. 535). Hence Ian Norrie's verdict that the paperback revolution 'gained pace' in the fifties.[19] Indeed, in 1955 Kurt Enoch was to claim that 'Editorially the gap between mass and class publishing has narrowed strikingly' (*BPA*, p. 548). The paperback revolution, plainly a stimulus to growth, was in turn accompanied by expanding demand in the education sector; again the Second World War was a catalyst, since 'Shortly after the war . . . returned servicemen began to crowd the colleges at the government's expense . . .' (*BPA*, p. 401).

These changes can fairly be seen to be critical, given the publishing industry's very high origination and indivisible costs (for manuscript-reading, editing, sub-editing, setting, proof-reading, and so on). One illustration is provided by C. Pratten and R. M. Dean in their book *The Economies of Large-Scale Production in British Industry*.[20] Pratten and Dean treat with the UK publishing scene, but for the purposes of this discussion their analysis holds good transatlantically, and it is particularly useful as its data was mostly compiled in 1961. They demonstrate that, in the printing industry in the early sixties, indivisibles typically accounted for well over half the production cost per unit (*ELP*, p. 27). This, combined with other high publishing indivisibles, meant that enormous savings could result from extended print-runs, provided sales proved to be high. This provides a key context for the emergence of the blockbuster complex. For example, in 1961, if the unit cost of a print-run of 1000 copies were to be regarded as 100, then the unit cost of a print-run of 50,000 would be only 8, a saving of 92 units (*ELP*, p. 29). Technological changes accentuated this: long print-runs better justified the use of rotary printers: at full capacity, costs could be reduced by approximately 27 per cent, and big rotary printers in turn could be as much as 42 per cent cheaper to operate than small rotaries (*ELP*, p. 33). Pratten and Dean then point out that paperbacks are a particular case in point: 'From the earlier discussion of the economies of scale resulting from larger editions and from using rotary machines, we can appreciate how the printing of paperbacks can achieve economies, often to a significant degree' (*ELP*, p. 35). Paperbacks reduce the indivisible cost of binding, and justify bigger print runs either because they are already proven sales successes or, as with quality paperbacks, are cheaper initially per unit (*ELP*, p. 35). A consequence of all this is the conclusion that: 'The most obvious economies of scale . . . are associated with increasing the size of printing orders' (*ELP*, p. 39). Michael Lane draws a compelling portrait of how publishers were forced by these pressures in the post-war period to take on board new marketing and market-research strategies: 'new patterns of business organisation' were required by a trade that was 'now part of the communications industry'.[21] Inevitably, 'With planned expansion requiring additional capital, consideration [was] given to "going public"' (*BPA*, pp. 401–2).

By the late fifties, however, I wish to argue, new stresses were beginning to accrue, as the other elements of the communications industry, and in particular television, began to prevail in the consumer-spending arena. It was at this time that Bernard Geis published the first film and television tie-ins, at Prentice Hall in 1957 and under his own imprint later in the fifties (*BC*, p. 24). The much-expanded, heavily capitalised publishing houses thus increasingly adopted the solutions offered by mergers and flotations. The earlier trends now became decisive; James T. Farrell, writing in 1946, can be cast as prophetic: 'the tendency towards combinations and concentrations in the book industry . . . will increase the difficulties of operation for small and independent publishers'.[22] As Madison puts it, 'In the late 1950s and early 1960s merging and going public became contagious' (*BPA*, p. 402). It was precisely in this climate, at this transition point, when the process of conglomeration was accelerating, that Grove Press was founded, a small independent publisher that by 1959 could fairly be described as 'struggling' (*EO*, p. 69).

Grove Press, at the time a nascent publishing house, was purchased in 1952 by Barney Rosset for $3000. Throughout its first decade the press lost money steadily and 'was often on the brink of bankruptcy'.[23] Rosset kept the enterprise afloat by recourse to his personal fortune, for he had inherited over $1 million from his father, but this private fund was a finite source of capital. During this period Grove Press established a reputation through its pronounced interest in the *avant-garde*, and in particular the European *avant-garde*.[24] However, in 1959 Grove took the obviously risky step, for a precariously funded publishing house, of openly publishing the unexpurgated text of *Lady Chatterley's Lover*. This was an action premeditatedly prepared for: from as early as 1954 Rosset had been in correspondence with Frieda Lawrence concerning the possibility, and both clearly knew that what would occur would be a 'battle'.[25] Rosset had also secured the support of a number of distinguished American academics, including Jacques Barzun and Mark Schorer (*EO*, pp. 68–9). Indeed the latter was to contribute a scholarly article in 1957 to what was, in effect, Grove

Press's in-house literary review, *Evergreen Review* (though in many respects its *avant-garde* predilections allied it to contemporary little magazines).[26] This article served both as a critical estimation and a piece of textual research, detailing Schorer's work on the three extant manuscripts of Lady Chatterley. Plainly, given the dearth of such scholarly commentaries elsewhere in *Evergreen*, Schorer's essay was intended as further defensive preparation.

There need be no doubt that Grove's, and Rosset's, commitment to overthrowing censorship constraints was real, even if Rosset was to admit, disarmingly, that he took up the fight 'to make money' (*BPA*, p. 535). When the battle was finally won, in 1959, Evergreen duly celebrated, describing Judge Frederick Van Pelt Bryan's verdict as 'an important – even historic – step forward in the long struggle against literary censorship in this country'.[27] Rosset himself was a declared opponent of censorship.[28] Such an observation goes along with the usual verdict on Grove: that it was (and is) a 'serious' publishing house, committed to the publication of 'good' literature, implicitly or explicitly contrasted with others whose primary motive is financial gain.[29] Such a binary division is again and again encountered in critical examinations of the publishing industry. Pierre Bourdieu has, I feel crucially, proposed that such a distinction is more arbitrary than substantial. In an important essay that in part focuses on the publishing industry, 'La Production de la croyance: contribution à une économie des biens symboliques', Bourdieu proposes that such categorisation, whilst correctly identifying the orientation of the more commercial publishing houses towards rapid accumulation of capital, fails to recognise that those publishers whose orientation is less obviously commercial are still concerned with profit and loss: their expectations are longer-term, their financial estimations of eventual profitability tied up with the accumulation of long-term profits, what he terms 'symbolic capital'.[30] In some ways, Grove Press provides an excellent illustration of this thesis. One might begin by noticing that Bourdieu takes as his main example of the acquisition of 'symbolic capital' the publication by Editions de Minuit of Samuel Beckett's *En attendant Godot* in 1952, and that it was, in fact, Grove Press that first published *Waiting for Godot* in America, in 1954.

More central, however, is the observation that Grove's adoption of a series of allegedly obscene authors – Lawrence, Miller, Genet, Burroughs, de Sade, Selby – meant that, in Bourdieu's terms, immediate profits became available whilst symbolic capital also accrued. The infamy of the texts involved, combined with inevitable US censorship problems, created spectacular best-seller sales in the short term, whilst the potential for longer-term sales continued to exist. The figures are dramatic, and the conclusion inescapable, for 'The various editions of *Lady Chatterley's Lover* that came out in 1959 and 1960 sold over six million copies' (*EO*, p. 120). Ian Norrie describes the phenomenon entertainingly: 'Lorries stopped outside bookshops with engines throbbing, as rough-handed drivers strode inside to buy *Lady Chatterley* . . . .'[31] Rembar sums it up when he observes that 'The average man, it was pretty clear, was buying [*Lady Chatterley*] because it was a dirty book' (*EO*, p. 120).

Grove's serious approach succeeded in deflecting the threat of censorship, as Judge Bryan's opinion in 1959 demonstrates: 'No one is naïve enough to think Grove Press did not expect to profit from the book. Nevertheless, the format and promotional material, and the whole approach to publication, treat the book as a serious work of literature' (*EO*, p. 486). Rembar gets close to identifying the problem when speaking of the 'inverted snobbism' that renders a text more vulnerable to censorship if published in a cheap paperback edition (*EO*, p. 172). The realities of the acquisition of symbolic capital are exposed in the care with which Grove sought to preserve its 'serious' reputation whilst also clearly seeking to resolve its own capitalisation dilemmas. As D. H. Lawrence expresses it, 'The monstrous lie of money lurks under the cloak of purity.'[32]

The dramatic sales figures achieved by *Lady Chatterley* were to be reproduced when Henry Miller's *Tropic of Cancer* had struggled through its travails: here Grove Press guarded its investment by supporting booksellers in over sixty prosecutions (*EO*, p. 168ff.). Putnam's similarly benefited from the successful defence of *Fanny Hill*. The allure of the censored/recently decensored text for readers can be accounted for by appeal to a concept formulated by Walter Benjamin in his essay 'The Work of Art in an Age of Mechanical Reproduction'.[33] Benjamin here proposed that the work of art, prior to the invention of mechanical reproduction processes, possessed an 'aura' (WA, p. 223). Benjamin in part reached this conclusion, as he states in 'Unpacking my Library', through his status as a 'genuine [book] collector' who was therefore concerned with 'genuineness' and 'origin'.[34] The problem is that this 'authenticity' becomes jeopardised in the process of mechanical reproduction because 'the quality of the original['s] . . . presence is always depreciated' and this in turn means that 'that which withers in the age of mechanical reproduction is the aura of the work of art' (WA, p. 223). Benjamin relates these ideas mostly to photography and film. Literature is hardly mentioned, because 'The enormous changes which printing, the mechanical reproduction of writing, has brought about in literature are a familiar story' (WA, p. 220). Pornographic literature, I would maintain, has in contrast been relatively neglected as a category, and here mechanical reproduction's intervention has been less decisive: censored books are not readily available, and therefore the depreciation of authenticity must be less: the 'aura' is relatively well preserved. If this be conceded, censored pornography as an art form can be regarded, in Benjamin's phrase, as more akin to 'ritual' than other forms of literature (WA, p. 226). There is a difficulty here, since the term 'ritual' is not well defined. In part, 'ritual' is 'the location of [the work of art's] original use value' (WA, p. 226), which places it in 'the domain of tradition' (WA, p. 223). But Benjamin is also (more usefully, for my purposes) in part referring to the sacred, near-magical cult qualities that the authentic original art-work possesses for its audience in 'the quality of its presence' (WA, p. 223).

What I would suggest, then, is that this quality of censored pornography is a main source of its startling appeal, because it holds out a promise of authenticity, which Benjamin describes as 'the authority of the object' (WA, p. 223). As he puts it, 'Today the cult value would seem to demand that the work of art remain hidden' (WA, p. 227). Censorship, if only incidentally, effects this. Once decensorship occurs, however, the promise of such authority will be steadily eroded, but Benjamin goes on to observe that this erosion is not to be lamented, a point to which I shall return. In the short term, however, 'auratic' qualities continue to inhere, and sales are consequently enormous. It is my contention that the anti-censorship campaigns of Grove Press, Putnam's and others need therefore to be placed in the context of publishing's capitalisation dilemmas in the mid twentieth century, and need to be seen as a cashing-in on the auratic authority of the freshly decensored, which represented a short-term resolution to the problem. Rosset's eagerness to publish forbidden texts has to be viewed in the context of Grove's financial losses. What remains to be answered, of course, is why publishers' assaults on censorship in the late fifties and early sixties should have so rapidly and successfully revised and diluted the discourse of censorship.

The standard answer here is to make reference to changing social values, and to argue that what was unacceptable in previous decades became acceptable in the period 1959 to 1966. This obviously historicist explanation poses several problems, however. It is patently untrue that over time moral standards have consistently become more liberal, and to appeal to dominant social values as the arbiter of censorship practices is quickly, and unsurprisingly, revealed as echoing in one's argument the dominant discourse of censorship, invoking, as it does, patent offensiveness and redeeming social values as criteria for assessing the acceptability of art at any time. Rembar falls into precisely this pattern, attributing changes in the laws to related changes in, as he terms it, 'general' attitudes (*EO*, p. 87). Yet, later in the same book he stresses that it was 'not the will of the people' that 'saved these books' (*EO*, p. 174). An unhappy fissure exists here; and we must notice that Rembar's early invocation of changes in 'general attitude' more or less echoes the words of Justice Brennan in the Roth opinion, when he spoke of 'the outer limits of tolerance imposed by the standards of the community in these present times' (*EO*, p. 133). To argue 'changing standards' is virtually to conduct the debate within the terms laid down by the censors themselves. Surely a more fundamental question has to be addressed: just why the erotic should be classified as in some way equivalent to the political in terms of capitalist society's determination to censor it, and why this resolve became so subdued in the mid twentieth century.

A near-contemporaneous analysis provided by Herbert Marcuse in *Eros and Civilization*[35] can be usefully adapted here. Marcuse suggests, in a rereading of Freud, that 'sexuality [is] . . . an essentially explosive force in "conflict" with civilization . . . an inevitable . . . conflict between pleasure principle and reality principle, between sexuality and civilization' (*EC*, pp. 38–9). In this way 'Civilization plunges [us] into a destructive dialectic: the perpetual restrictions on Eros ultimately weaken the life instinct and thus strengthen and release the . . . forces . . . of destruction', thereby creating what Marcuse calls 'surplus-repression' (*EC*, p. 40). As a result, in 'advanced capitalist society' there is a need for 'release from repression', and one form this can take is

'repressive desublimation': release of sexuality in modes and forms which reduce and weaken erotic energy . . . the Reality Principle extends its hold over Eros. The most telling illustration is provided by the methodical introduction of sexiness into business, politics, propaganda, etc. To the degree to which sexuality obtains a definite sales value . . . it is itself transformed into an instrument of social cohesion.   (*EC*, pp. xi–x)

I would suggest that the mid-century anti-censorship campaigns of publishers, and in particular Grove Press, are usefully viewed in this light. If they are so viewed, then Marcuse's subsequent strictures are plainly germane. He goes on to maintain that identifying this 'familiar trend' towards providing sexuality with a definite sales value 'illuminate[s] the gap which separates even the possibilities of liberation from the established state of affairs' (*EC*, p. x). It is therefore consistent with Marcuse's argument for me to suggest that mid-twentieth-century reductions in censorship, occurring at the very time (1961) when Marcuse wrote his Preface, demonstrate his argument that

one can practice non-repressiveness within the framework of the established society. . . . But . . . this sort of protest turns into a vehicle of stabilization and even conformity, because it not only leaves the roots of the evil untouched, but also testifies to the personal liberties that are practicable within the framework of general repression.   (*EC*, p. ix)

One can thus argue that the ability to release the energies of the erotic into the processes of selling, so realising its sales value, required a slackening of censorship, and that Grove's underlying commercial motivations in its anti-censorship crusade are in themselves, by extension, illustrative of this thesis. For this reason, I would maintain, the discourse of censorship adopted the distinction between 'hardcore' pornography, seen as irredeemably viscious, and 'softcore' pornography or writing 'with redeeming social importance', regarded as permissible. The tensions created by repressing the Pleasure Principle, Marcuse argues, are thereby contained.

It is tempting to adopt this post-Freudian perspective wholesale, since it locates the obviously nebulous concept of changing social value in specific changes in social practice that do not rely on vague claims for liberalisation. However, despite Marcuse's claim that both Freud and he conceived of a society that could solve the double-bind of the 'destructive dialectic' created by 'the perpetual restrictions on Eros' (*EC*, p. 40), I myself want to draw back from the rather deterministic trace running through his presentation of repressive desublimation as simply serving to increase social cohesion. And here I wish once again to appeal to Walter Benjamin's analysis in 'The Work of Art in the Age of Mechanical Reproduction', where he proposes that, once the work of art loses its aura, and hence its 'parasitical dependence on ritual', art 'begins to be based in another practice – politics' (*WA*, p. 226). If my argument that censorship artificially preserves aura can be accepted, then decensorship transfers the erotic/pornographic from the realm of ritual to the practice of politics, an argument which anyway would preserve some consistency with Marcuse's analysis of the abuse of the erotic in repressive desublimation, since the latter is also seen quite plainly as ideological. What now becomes possible, then, is the 'politicisation' of the erotic/pornographic (*WA*, p. 244). And that, I would claim, is precisely what we have seen occurring since the mid sixties.

Perhaps the history of *Evergreen Review* can illustrate this process. Initially the review was used quite instrumentally by Grove to strengthen its hand in its anti-censorship campaign.[36] However, after Rembar had declared an end to obscenity, the review continued to focus upon aspects of sexuality and the erotic in its pages; but now this focus was unambiguously linked to its financial travails.[37] This led in turn to disputes with its contributors, and with the growing women's liberation movements in New York. These took offence at the uses to which the review put the erotic and sexuality. The recurring debate reached a climax when several of *Evergreen Review*'s contributing editors resigned within a few months of each other in 1970.[38] Obviously, these disputes were part of a larger debate, with gathered momentum in the late sixties, about portraits of sexuality and the uses of the erotic: whereas previously censorship had been at the core of the political controversy, eroticism and its uses now assumed centre-stage in a clear process of 'politicisation' of the erotic, once it had unambiguously entered the age of mechanical reproduction. Benjamin's final words therefore assume a new, extended authority: once art has become based in the practice of politics, the Left must 'respond . . . by politicizing art' (*WA*, p. 244) or, in this case, the erotic.

Plainly the end of obscenity had not arrived: the period analysed by Rembar had rather seen the transfer of emphasis from repression to exploitation, a transfer incidentally promoted by Grove's search for auratic blockbusters to solve its publishing capitalisation crisis, and ultimately facilitated by capitalism's desire to channel less restrictedly repressive desublimation into the processes of modern marketing. The legal breakthroughs of this period need to be viewed within these contexts, and the new terrain of the debate about the erotic must be clearly identified. Erotic art, like all art, has of course always been interlinked with politics. Benjamin is, however, claiming (by implication, if my argument be accepted) that erotic art is now itself *politicised*. The erotic text, no longer a guarantor of auratic authenticity, shrouded by the laws of obscenity, becomes instead plainly available as a representational discourse, a deployment of signifiers within contemporary culture in an age of mechanical reproduction, potentially tending towards objectification (relationships of syntactical power) or towards the restoration of mutuality to sexuality and gender relations. Notions of hard versus soft pornography are quite beside the point. But this becomes another line of argument, within which, for example, *The Naked Lunch*, in its satiric, forensic interrogation of the structure of power relations in objectified sexual activity in Interzone (the area where bondage and sadism are linked to capital punishment), might be represented as a protest against all processes of objectification in sexual interaction, as distinct from the obscene exploitative subversion of desire's potential for endless mutuality.[39]

NOTES

For source abbreviations see notes 1 (*EO*), 13 (*BC*), 16 (*BPA*), 20 (*ELP*), 33 (*WA*), 35 (*EC*).

1. Charles Rembar, *The End of Obscenity* (London: André Deutsch, 1969). Page references in text, prefixed *EO*.
2. P. R. MacMillan, *Censorship and Public Morality* (Aldershot: Gower, 1983).
3. Norman St John Stevas, *Obscenity and the Law* (London: Secker and Warburg, 1956).
4. Antonio Gramsci, *The Prison Notebooks* (1929–35), tr. Quintin Hoare and Geoffrey Nowell Smith (London: Lawrence and Wishart, 1971) p. 55ff.; Louis Althusser, 'Ideology and the Ideological State Apparatus', in *Lenin and Philosophy and Other Essays*, tr. Ben Brewster (New

York: Monthly Review Press, 1971). In the latter, the Repressive State Apparatus is described as including the courts, and the Ideological State Apparatus as including 'the legal ISA' (p. 143); earlier in the same essay, when defining the two 'instances' in the 'superstructure', Althusser had spoken of 'the politico-legal (law and the State) and ideology (the different ideologies, religious, ethical, legal, political, etc.)' (p. 134). Gramsci similarly places law and the legal system at a nexus point between the state and civil society: 'If every State tends to create and maintain a certain type of civilization and of citizen . . . and to eliminate certain customs and attitudes and to disseminate others, then the Law will be its instrument for this purpose (together with . . . other institutions and activities)' (*Prison Notebooks*, p. 246).

5. D. H. Lawrence, *Lady Chatterley's Lover* (New York: Grove Press, 1959); Henry Miller, *Tropic of Cancer* (New York: Grove Press, 1961); Hubert Selby, *Last Exit to Brooklyn* (New York: Grove Press, 1964); Pauline Reage, *The Story of O* (New York: Grove Press, 1966); William Burroughs, *The Naked Lunch* (New York: Grove Press, 1962).

6. John Cleland, *Memoirs of a Woman of Pleasure* (New York: Putnam's, 1965).

7. *Evergreen Review*, 9, no. 36 (1965) 40.

8. Burroughs, *The Naked Lunch*, pp. 117–18 (suspension points are Burroughs').

9. Ibid., p. 1ff.

10. Serge Grunberg, *A la recherche d'un corps* (Paris: Editions du Seuil, 1979) p. 37.

11. Pierre Macherey, *Towards a Theory of Literary Production* (French original, 1966), tr. Geoffrey Wall (London: Routledge and Kegan Paul, 1978).

12. Quoted in MacMillan, *Censorship and Public Morality*, p. vii.

13. Thomas Whiteside, *The Blockbuster Complex: Conglomerates, Show Business, and Book Publishing* (Middletown, Conn.: Weslyan University Press, 1981). Page references in text, prefixed *BC*.

14. Michael Lane, *Books and Publishers: Commerce against Culture in Postwar Britain* (Lexington, Mass.: Lexington Books, 1980) p. 7.

15. Raymond Williams, *The Long Revolution* (London: Chatto and Windus, 1961) p. 170ff. and *passim*.

16. Charles A. Madison, *Book Publishing in America* (New York: McGraw-Hill, 1966). Further references in text, prefixed *BPA*.

17. Lewis A. Coser, Charles Kadushin and Walter W. Powell, *Books: The Culture and Commerce of Publishing* (New York: Basic Books, 1982) p. 20ff.

18. Philip Unwin, 'Epilogue 1960–1975', in Stanley Unwin, *The Truth about Publishing*, 8th edn (London: Allen and Unwin, 1976) p. 242.

19. Ian Norrie, *Mumby's Publishing and Bookselling in the Twentieth Century*, 6th edn (London: Bell and Hyman, 1982) p. 160.

20. C. Pratten and R. M. Dean, *The Economics of Large-Scale Production in British Industry: An Introductory Study* (Cambridge: Cambridge University Press, 1965). Page references in text, prefixed *ELP*.

21. Lane, *Books and Publishers*, pp. 51ff., 65, 70.

22. James T. Farrell, 'Will the Commercialization of Publishing Destroy

Good Writing?', *New Directions*, 9 (1946) 6–7. It was precisely these pressures on small commercial publishing houses, I would argue, that led to the growth in size and scope of non-commercial, usually *avant-garde*, small presses.

23. Gerald Jonas, 'The Story of Grove', *New York Times*, 21 Jan 1968, section 6, p. 48. Much of my account of Grove Press is drawn from this article. The rest is drawn from my own research, detailed in my unpublished PhD thesis: '*Evergreen Review* (1957–1973) and its Relationship to Contemporary American Culture' (University of Exeter, 1977).

24. See Jonas, *passim*.

25. Frieda Lawrence, letter to Barney Rosset, 4 Dec 1954, Grove Press Files, series VI, Part Bi, George Arendt Research Library, Syracuse University, NY.

26. *Evergreen Review*, 1, no. 1 (1957) 149–78.

27. *Evergreen Review*, 3 (1959) 38.

28. Jonas, in *New York Times*, 21 Jan 1968, section 6, p. 48.

29. See Coser *et al.*, *Books*, p. 36ff.

30. Pierre Bourdieu, 'La production de la croyance: contribution à une économie des biens symboliques', *Actes de la Recherche en Sciences Sociales*, 13 (Feb 1977) 23ff. See also, for a discussion of this, Coser *et al.*, *Books*, p. 44ff.

31. Norrie, *Mumby's Publishing*, p. 182.

32. D. H. Lawrence, 'Pornography and Censorship' (1929), quoted in Stephen Spender, 'Thoughts on Censorship in the World', in *Censorship: Fifty Years of Conflict* (New York: Oxford University Press, 1964) p. 117.

33. Walter Benjamin, 'The Work of Art in an Age of Mechanical Reproduction' (1936), in *Illuminations*, tr. Harry Zohn (London: Jonathan Cape, 1970) pp. 219–53. Individual page references in text, prefixed WA.

34. Benjamin, *Illuminations*, p. 44.

35. Herbert Marcuse, *Eros and Civilization* (1952; New York: Vintage Books, 1962). Page references in text, prefixed EC.

36. See Ellis, '*Evergreen Review* (1957–1973)', p. 214ff.

37. Ibid., p. 310ff.

38. Ibid., p. 331ff.

39. See Susanne Kappeler, *The Pornography of Representation* (Oxford: Polity Press, 1986), for some recent approaches to this debate, as developed by Bernard Williams and Susan Barrowclough.

4

Feature-length Sex Films

ANTHONY CRABBE

The recent interest in sex books and films has generated some fierce controversies about how this material is to be understood. So far, the bulk of this analysis has concentrated upon theoretical definition of what sexual representation is. Whilst this is a useful approach, there does seem to be a risk that commentators will concentrate on the theoretical issues at the expense of practical analysis of the material they are discussing. Accordingly, I think there is room for a more practical approach in which the material may be examined in its historical context. Such an approach cannot be offered as a replacement for theoretical perspectives, but rather as a complement to them. Nevertheless, in proposing the need of a more historical approach, it is first necessary to discuss the limitations of the theoretical one.

Sexual activity has been represented in the art of most cultures since their first emergence. In Greek pottery and Indian temples, sex appears to have been simply one subject among many. It is only in recent Western culture that a distinction has come to be drawn between two supposedly different kinds of sexual representation: pornographic and erotic.

The controversy turns around two distinct and yet inseparable questions. The first concerns how each may be defined. The second question concerns the effect that each has on its audience.

One of the earliest expositions of the first question was occasioned by the work of D. H. Lawrence, particularly by the novel *Lady Chatterley's Lover*. In 1928, Lawrence sought to defend the legitimacy of his London exhibition of paintings by pointing to the absence of artistic merit in pornographic material. To this day, artistic merit remains a key criterion for distinguishing the two, as in the British Williams Report of 1978, which describes erotic literature as

art on a sexual theme related specifically to emotions rather than merely actions, and sexual depictions which are justifiable on

44

aesthetic ground. . . . [The difference between eroticism and pornography] is the difference between celebratory and mastur-batory sex.[1]

Leaving aside the adequacy of such definitions for the moment, we must remember that the Williams Report was the product of national concern about the effects of sexually explicit material on society at large. Indeed, for some sections at this time, such as the women's movement, the *effect* of pornography came to be its defining characteristic. Consider, for instance, the feminist slogan 'Pornography is the theory, rape is the practice', or Kate Millett's claim 'Pornography *is* violence towards women.'[2]

Unfortunately, the Williams Report itself indicates how difficult it is to establish concrete evidence which would support this view. Nevertheless, this does not rule out the attempt to define pornography in terms of its ideological effects: 'Male power is the *raison d'être* of pornography: the degradation of the female is the means of achieving this power.'[3] Although this is a less concrete approach, it has allowed for wider agreement about the nature of pornography. Indeed, such a view seems to be taken for granted in much current literature, which has moved on to discuss whether pornography is a cause of ideological malaise, or one of its symptoms.[4]

This recent shifting of ground from concrete to ideological definition of pornography actually makes the examination of specific instances of it a more complicated matter. It raises the questions of whether such an ideology is itself a concrete thing, whether it can be satisfactorily identified, and then whether such an ideology might predispose certain individuals towards particular responses to sexual material and so forth. Because of the huge difficulties such questions raise, it seems best for the purpose of this brief survey to start from the inside and work out: that is to say, to analyse the material in its historical context and try to see what understandings contemporary audiences might have. I leave it to others to evaluate my speculations within a wider context if they wish.

In order to work within these limits, I propose to dispense with the distinction between pornography and erotica. As Andrea Dworkin points out, the term 'pornography' is itself perjorative in meaning, being first coined in the nineteenth century to describe the depiction of the most despised of human creatures – prostitutes.[5]

However, Dworkin goes on to argue that this is then a definitive description of the attitudes towards women found in pornography. In fact, this is no argument at all: it is simply an assertion that, when I find material which debases women, I call it 'pornography'. It might be the case that material of the same type does not debase women, or that people cannot agree about what debasing women means – in which case, we are still left with an unresolved definition.

The present sense of 'erotica' is another legacy of the nineteenth century, a period when scholars seemed to have felt obliged to use euphemisms, preferably constructed out of a dead language, to describe the living menace of sexual arousal. Although a less perjorative term than pornography, 'erotica' seems just as ineffective. As Morse Peckham has argued, to claim that 'erotica' has intrinsic artistic merit is merely to beg the question of what that merit is.[6] This in effect, is to pre-empt the response that *any* viewer might have. Regrettably, Peckham goes on to propose his own definitions, which seems to be a denial of his own best argument.

The Williams Report definitions present a slightly different case because they seek to *impose* a consensus view in order to permit legislation which protects society at large. This may be a necessary political evil, but it is dangerous as a critical approach. Were critics to adopt such definitions, they might well find themselves forwarding a kind of Leavisite view that the critic's job is to define the responses which a 'perceptive' audience *ought* to have. Critics are not legislators, although many of them try to be. The following example may illustrate the dangers of working with legislative definitions.

As a schoolboy I got hold of a widely circulated copy of *Lady Chatterley's Lover*, which fell open immediately to reveal the 'mucky' passages in the book. The degree of wear to some pages and not others revealed that sixth-formers were no respectors of Lawrence's artistic intentions. Indeed, the common practice of reading the novel in hidden corners indicates that it provoked masturbatory activity despite the conviction of those like Lawrence that this was a characteristic effect of pornography.

Some may argue that this only demonstrates that seventeen-year-olds are unsuitable critics of erotica. But this is a dangerously elitist argument which ignores the capacity of the same audience to respond sensitively to a novel such as *Tess of the d'Urbervilles*. It might even be argued on this basis that *Lady Chatterley's Lover* is really a pornographic novel after all. I do not even wish to consider such a view here because the whole issue of what a work of art 'is' – the issue of its 'natural' status – seems to be a red herring. It interposes itself between critics and their material, distorting their judgment of what they *do* see with concern about what they think they *ought* to see.

The discarding of the terms 'pornography' and 'erotica' helps to remove such obstacles and instead focuses attention on straightforward description. In both cases this relates to subject matter that is predominantly concerned with the representation of sexual activity. In everyday language, such representations are often called 'sex films', 'sex books' and so forth, which seems a perfectly adequate description of what an audience would expect to find depicted in them. Furthermore, this approach is in keeping with the way other labels are used: we do not find critics trying to redefine the detective genre just because Raymond Chandler writes better than Mickey Spillane.

The adoption of a purely descriptive label helps us to place sex films in their context much more easily. It is true that most of them are ridiculously poor stuff – but then so are many TV soap operas, 'video nasties' and Mills and Boom romances, all of which have been argued by various commentators to be 'pornographic' in their way. It surely matters little whether they are or not, the significant issue being that they are, like sex films, examples of 'popular art'. That is to say, all are representations produced for the mass entertainment market. In particular I want to investigate featurelength sex films which were made for display in public cinemas and cinema clubs in the 1960s and 1970s.

These were films made in Europe and America which first appeared publicly on the crest of the 'permissive' wave of the 1960s. They fall into two categories: 'skinflicks', in which the sexual activity is comprised mainly of nude display and simulated sex; and 'hardcore' films, in which the cast participate in actual sex. The sense of 'hardcore' here should not be confused with the other common use of the label to describe 'specialist' material devoted to sado-masochism, animal sex and so forth, much of which is illegal and sold 'under the counter'.

Short hardcore films known as 'loops' have been made since the turn of the century, mostly by non-professional 'chancers' evading censorship laws and usually in small-film format. Formerly they could only be viewed in private and domestic venues, but following the decensorship which swept the West in the 1960s it became possible for the general public to walk off the street into cinemas or shops to see such films.

Decensorship also saw the rapid growth of skinflicks, which were mostly made by experienced film-makers using professional casts and crews at a time when the traditional film industry was in sharp decline. Such films took advantage of censorial relaxation to 'beef up' their sexual situations, which would have been presented in a much less bold way before. Thus in *Au Pair Girls* we find the shy boy and sensitive oriental girl who fall in love, and the clumsy boy who gets marooned in a bar with a sexy Swede, and so on, all presented in a fairly explicit manner.

Feature-length hardcores first appeared in the early 1970s and were initially made by the loop industry. However, many, such as the American *Behind the Green Door* and the Danish *Under the Sign of . . .* series, saw a fusion of the loop and skinflick industries, where the technical demands of feature-film making required the skills of the traditional industry. It also became common practice to make as many as three versions of such films as *Through the Looking Glass*. One version was hardcore and the other two were altered or cut to meet differing local censorship laws, enabling them to be exhibited in ordinary cinemas.

The cross-overs between these various genres are nothing new in the history of popular entertainment. In imperial Rome, for instance, the bawdy satyr plays of ancient Greece combined with the 'spectacles' of the Roman games to produce shows in which adulterous episodes were actually performed by the players and stand-in 'players' (convicted criminals) were really mutilated and executed in the manner required by the plot. In their most popular form such shows involved the re-enactment of a myth – a story familiar to all: thus Prometheus might be seen having his liver torn out by a trained eagle, or Orpheus, who was supposed to be able to tame wild beasts with his music, might be seen failing and being torn apart by them instead.

This is not the place to inquire how Roman citizens could find entertainment in such spectacles, but it is a fact that most did – even if they viewed them as 'vulgar' and accorded actors the disdain in which pornographers are held by most people nowadays. It has also been commonly agreed that the Roman games served as an instrument of social control and manipulation.[7] In particular, they have been seen as a means of diverting the constant threat of public disorder brought about by unpopular policies, factional rivalry and so forth.

Here there are direct links with contemporary times. The decensorship which facilitated the growth of publicly viewable sex films was not the result of government bounty. In legal terms, it resulted from a series of bitter and protracted trials throughout the West. In Britain these trials challenged censorship laws dating back to 1857. I do not believe it is possible fully to understand the nature of the specific films discussed below unless one has some understanding of the decensorship which made them possible.

The principal challenger of censorship was the entertainment industry. Though its representatives it lobbied parliaments and funded the numerous 'experts' who testified to the beneficial effects of books such as *Lady Chatterley's Lover*, shows such as *Oh, Calcutta!*, and so on. The industry itself was responding to a growing demand for more 'honest', 'adult' material, stimulated by the widespread desire to overthrow the puritanical public standards of the Victorian age.

Indeed, many political radicals in the 1960s came to adopt sexual liberation as a means for effecting social and political revolution. It is not easy to summarise the numerous variants of this tendency, but, generally speaking, most extended a psychoanalytical view of the individual to the collective state. They argued along the lines that censorship and political repression produced harmful social effects which paralleled the effects of repression in the individual. More sophisticated versions of this view helped to fuel the student radicalism in France which led to the riots there in May 1968. In Scandinavia there were provocative spectacles of public nudity and sex. In America and Britain there were hippy festivals and 'love-ins' conducted under the now-legendary slogan 'Turn on, tune in, drop out.'

Such groups repeatedly tested the censors with their 'underground' literature. One of the most notorious cases concerned the 'school kids' issue of the magazine *Oz* in 1971. In the longest-ever obscenity trial in Britain, the prosecution case turned on an attempt to establish the obscenity of items such as a bawdy version of the Rupert Bear cartoon-strip. Yet we might feel that it was the actual views of the school-age contributors which most alarmed the censors. Consider for instance the demands of 'Anne', a teenager still under parental care: 'Freedom of sexual expression in public has many tight restrictions. One may kiss in certain places but only fuck in a few places at certain times. Surely this idea is as pretentious and puritanical as the old forms of censorship?'[8]

Although the censors did eventually relinquish many of their powers through court hearings and Acts of Parliament, we may see their withdrawal as tactical and limited. Far better to let *Penthouse* show pubic hair to the public in the privacy of their own homes than let them see the exposed genitalia of stoned hippies basking in the greenery of a public park. Better to let the public view an orgy in the seclusion of a decaying cinema than watch or join the hippies in the park in a 'love-in'. It was safer to have the public satisfying their prurience rather than their conscience, expending their energies on masturbation rather than agitation, watching a revolution rather than executing it.

In many respects, decensorship was a return to the policy of the Roman circus. Bear in mind that the moral basis of nineteenth-century censorship lay in the principles of the Christian Church. This was the same establishment which in late Roman times exacted censorial revenge upon the circuses where their founding fathers had been so horribly destroyed, and the mime plays where the faith had often been mocked and its adherents actually crucified in savage burlesques.

In its need to exorcise the pagan past, the Christian Church came to develop a fundamentally different approach to sex. The pagans had acknowledged their sexuality – particularly its irrational aspects – by giving it a role in their everyday religion and art. So when the Church fathers sought to supplant paganism, they needed to redefine the significance of sexuality. This they did by castigating its irrational symptoms such as abandonment, licence and orgy, which had been celebrated in rites such as the Bacchanalia. Such irrational manifestations were portrayed as animal urges, unbecoming the higher nature of men. Pagan mythology had already represented the instinctive aspect of sex in, for instance, its tales of satyrs, those alarming but comical and endearing characters who cavorted on the public stages of the classical world. In Christian mythology, the satyr became the personification of the Devil himself. Sex came to be defined in exclusively rational terms as the act of procreation, which was the function of monogamous marriage.

Such a view persisted as the moral basis of that nineteenth-century censorship which was brought under attack in the 1960s and 1970s. The strategic withdrawal of the censors in that period had the effect of deflecting the political implications of sexual radicalism. By ceding power to the free market of the entertainment industry, the censors facilitated the runaway success of politically innocuous material such as *The Sensuous Woman*, *The Joy of Sex*, *Forum* and so forth. Such material preached a primarily sensual self-awareness, a liberation through private pleasure, as demonstrated by the blurb on the back cover of *The Sensuous Woman*:

> Every female has the ability and the right to be fully sensuous. But most women never learn how. *The Sensuous Woman* will show you how to attract a man worth your attention, drive him wild with pleasure, and keep him eagerly coming back for more. And *The Sensuous Woman* will show you how to reach peaks of erotic and loving pleasure you never dreamed were available to you. It instructs us, 'Learn to have a really joyous and fulfilling sex life.'[9]

By the late 1970s such an attitude seemed to many to be far from innocent but, on the contrary, an endorsement of a traditional kind of sexual politics. Earlier in the decade, though, the public was less concerned about the political aspects. They had little doubt that they were witness to a revolution – a revolution in what they could freely purchase. The backlash of the women's movement later on showed that not everyone subscribed to the lifestyle advocated by such products.

Decensorship allowed the economic muscle of the entertainment industry to transform freedom of expression into a consumable product. Consumers now acquired the sense of freedom to choose how to enjoy themselves, much as the Roman mob acquired the dubious freedom to satisfy their desires in aristocratically sponsored and state-subsidised games.

Decensorship kept open many small cinemas, which managed to limp through the seventies by specialising in sex films until they were finally dispatched by the home video in the eighties. And the Penthouse corporation, for instance, went from strength to strength, diversifying into films, gambling, scientific research and so forth which ultimately led to their endorsement of political candidates and political programmes. Such profuse and high-profile successes overshadowed the political implications of sexual liberation. The economic system forsaken by practitioners of sexual

liberation such as the hippies actually took over the public pro-
motion of liberation and by marketing it ensured its own
perpetuation.

These effects should not necessarily be viewed as evidence of a
calculated conspiracy, but should be seen rather as symptoms of
establishment confidence in the ultimate strength of its own
capitalist system, riding high in the 1960s. One is reminded the
arrogant confidence of the Romans in sanctioning excesses they
would surely not have tolerated in their subject states.

The first skinflick to achieve commercial and widespread popular
success was *Emmanuelle* (1973). Emmanuelle is the Sensuous
Woman brought to fictional life. She begins the film a repressed
and dissatisfied young wife, stranded at home in Paris whilst her
oil-executive husband is working and playing in Bangkok. He then
persuades her to join him and so she embarks upon her symbolic
voyage to liberation. Arriving from the dull grey of Paris, she finds
herself in the other-worldly splendour of a post-colonial Orient,
with its gracious native attendants, European clubs, sunshine and
so forth.

She soon discovers this paradise to be the land of the liberated,
where the affluent and beautiful flit like butterflies between sexual
liaisons that are common knowledge and seem to trouble no one.
In such an environment Emmanuelle manages to confide in her
husband about a disturbing sexual adventure during her flight.
This proves to his evident satisfaction that she is ripe for
induction. The rest of the plot concerns Emmanuelle's initiation
into an erotic way of life. Under her husband's benevolent eye she
is introduced to new and exotic kinds of sexual activity by members
of the liberated set. Starting with a grounding in spontaneous
masturbation by a teenage nymphette, Emmanuelle progresses to
lesbian dalliance with one woman, lesbian infatuation with another,
works her way up to heterosexual activity and finally graduates to
a gang-bang, supervised by a kind of sexual grand master selected
by her husband.

Following these rites of passage, the last frame of the film finds
her esconced in a womb-like cane chair, clad only in the silk print
of her new land and painted like a courtesan. Her calm betokens
the privacy of her new consciousness, whilst her arch gaze into

the camera torments the audience with the knowledge of delicious mysteries accessible only to the initiate.

The lure of this icon, which was used in posters for the film, gave a tremendous boost to the skinflick industry, which produced a spawn of imitations: among them, *Black Emmanuelle, Yellow Emmanuelle, Emily* and, of course, *Emmanuelle 2* and *3*. *Emmanuelle 2* (1975), sponsored by *Lui* magazine and with a different director, showed the progress of the fully fledged initiate.

Once again, we find Emmanuelle cruising the lush Orient. As the initiate she now adopts a masculine role, finding playmates of both sexes along the route from Hong Kong to Bali. As in the first film, exotic locations form the backdrops against which the plot unfolds. Luxury-class tourism provides the metaphor for pleasurable sexual wandering. The masculinised Emmanuelle is now a soulmate for her husband. They confide their adventures to each other, using them as stimuli for their own lovemaking, most notably when she tells him of how she had been mistaken for a whore by three sailors and had taken on all three simultaneously for money. However, she also rejects the advances of two men in the film, one she does not fancy and one she does, telling the latter that *she* decides who, when and where, thus depriving him of his traditional masculine role by assuming it herself.

Central to the plot is the discovery of a young virgin debutante, who is initiated as was Emmanuelle in the first film, by her and her husband. The story culminates in a threesome in which the girl is shared by husband and wife. The final frames show Emmanuelle rising from this melange to look once again into the camera.

This time the look signifies something rather different. It is more of a triumphant smile. Emmanuelle's sense of fulfilment lies not simply in her own liberation, as in the first film, but also in the induction of a convert. Through the activities of Emmanuelle and her ilk, the revolution in consciousness becomes infectious; even the tenderest virgins succumb.

The *Emmanuelle* films are a touchstone for feature-length sex films of this period. In part this is because their narrative themes recur with monotonous regularity in both skinflick and hardcore pictures. But mainly it is because the Emmanuelle character is the archetype of the masculinised pleasure-seeking female who haunts the fictions of seventies sex films. She devotes her time and money to self-fulfilment through sexual adventure, which becomes the goal of her affluent lifestyle. She is a woman 'more like a man' in the traditional sense.

At the same time as *Emmanuelle* was making headlines, the feature-length hardcore *Deep Throat* (1972) was on its way to becoming one of the biggest box office hits of the time. Made on a budget of $25,000, it grossed $50 million. It was made by a loop production company and directed by Gerard Damiano who had some background in conventional films. However, *Emmanuelle* was technically superior in every respect. Directed by Just Jaeckin, who had a successful career in photography behind him, *Emmanuelle* was carefully edited and scored, the sex discreetly simulated.

By contrast the celebrity of *Deep Throat* rested on its explicit depiction of numerous sexual feats, grainily photographed and repetitiously edited. Whilst it may have been technically superior to the loops of the time – its relative coarseness complemented the outrageous content – cinema audiences could feel the prurient thrill of watching in public perhaps the first blue movie many of them had seen. Even members of the Hollywood establishment such as Elizabeth Taylor and Sammy Davis Jr owned up to having seen the film; porn was suddenly chic.

As in *Emmanuelle*, the heroine of *Deep Throat*, played by Linda Lovelace, begins the film dissatisfied with her sex life. Then, with the help of a horny doctor, she discovers that she enjoys oral sex best of all because her clitoris is in her throat. To accommodate this remarkable fact, Linda is obliged to accommodate the whole penis in her mouth and throat. The episodic narrative of the film then permits her to display her other unusual abilities such as fucking herself with a large glass dildo and taking an entire fist in her vagina (in an earlier loop she had taken a girl's whole foot).

So the fantastic fictional premise of the film is a pretext for the presentation of sexual 'spectacle', entertaining in the manner of the explicit sex in Roman shows or the trick that dancers in wartime Cairo had of picking tips from the tables with their vaginas. In this respect, *Deep Throat* shows more 'real' sex than skinflicks such as *Emmanuelle*. The 'gimmick' of hardcore is the actual ability of the cast to perform unusual sexual feats for the camera.

However, this should not mislead us into believing that hardcore is the more 'realistic' genre. For one thing, it is very difficult to film the close tangle of sexual activity so that the viewer can see exactly what is happening. The technical artifice is just as great in hardcore as in, say, horror films, where gory special effects have to be laboriously constructed in order to provide the illusion of heads splitting open and the like.

Chuck Traynor, formerly Linda Lovelace's husband and manager, tells us in *Inside Linda Lovelace* (of which he seems to have been the true author) that only six penises were used in close up sequences in *Deep Throat*, although a dozen actors appeared to be doing the business.[10] According to Traynor, this is because it takes a special brand of man to be able to sustain an erection and perform under stop–start studio conditions. He claims that at least half the performers were homosexual and that most were exhibitionists.

These views tend to be supported by hardcore films such as *Exhibition* and *Behind the Scenes of a Blue Movie*. In the latter film there is an excruciating scene where a novice actor comes to his first intercourse scene and is completely unable to perform despite the patience of the crew and the manual and oral ministrations of his veteran partner. In *Exhibition* we see French actresses routinely coping with this problem, showing amusing Gallic *ennui*. In an issue of the magazine *Cinema Blue* there is a photograph showing even the seasoned team of Bent Weed and Dawn Cumming arousing a tired actor between scenes for the next take.[11] Furthermore, in hardcore films the moans, groans and dialogue during sex are invariably dubbed, often with hilarious consequences, as when actresses with full mouths are heard to cry 'Oh yeah', and so forth. In short, then, it requires all the cinematic devices of cutting, dubbing, editing and doubling to create the illusion of a continuous sexual performance. It can thus be seen that, even in this most basic respect, hardcore is as fictional, as dramatised as any other genre of popular cinema.

Despite its artistic crudity, *Deep Throat* does also work on a dramatic level. From a biological fantasy, it develops a fictional structure which allegorises the role of fellatio. The briefest survey of the popular literature of the period shows that attitudes about fellatio were altering radically. *The Sensuous Woman* says,

Does the idea of putting a man's penis in your mouth revolt you? If so, you are probably a typical product of current taboos against oral gratification. . . . Actually, kissing a man's penis is a lot less insanitary than kissing him on the mouth. . . . It never occurred to me that I would ever find oral sex fulfilling, but thanks to an explosive experience with a wildly uninhibited man, I finally tuned into the joys of oral gratification.[12]

The 'letters' pages of magazines such as *Forum* were filled with inquiries about the subject. In particular, they expressed fears about the possibility of disease and the dangers of swallowing sperm, and anxieties about the pleasurable gains for women and the best technique.

Deep Throat begins by justifying a woman's need to perform fellatio: her sex life is unsatisfactory without it. Then the film goes on to show what pleasure an adventurous woman (under medical supervision!) can derive from it and how, with some practice, she can give a man the ultimate pleasure. This is signified by the insertion of the *whole* penis into her mouth as well as by the fact that only when this is achieved can her ultimate pleasure be realised by the stimulation of her fantasy clitoris.

Of course, like so many allegories, this one too is built on the false premise of biological impossibility. Yet this is an artistically legitimate way of engaging the viewer's own imaginings and feelings. It helps the viewer to believe that fellatio is *mutually* rewarding and not, as is often argued, an exploitative form of male masturbation. This helps allay the male viewer's possible guilt as well as encourage his desire for fellatio as performed by an expert. For the female viewer it acts as a lesson that the ultimate pleasure for her is completely to satisfy a man, however egocentric his desires. Having said this, it is not clear that it means satisfying him *whatever* his desires. The episodes we see feature a lot of exhibitionism, but contain no violence or coercion; the heroine is too 'masculinised' for that to be necessary.

The expertise shown by Linda Lovelace in *Deep Throat* made her into a huge celebrity. Her publicity claimed that, next to Henry Kissinger, she was the most famous living American! *Emmanuelle*, likewise made an international star out of Sylvia Kristel, who was soon taking roles in traditional films such as *Airport '78*. Linda apparently had similar ambitions. Chuck Traynor makes her say, 'I worked for peanuts – or penises maybe – but I believed I would reach great heights. At least it seemed worth a try. Maybe it's that way with most of the girls.'[13]

Concerning the common notion that girls who worked in

hardcore were prostitutes, Traynor says, 'If money was the consideration, a girl would do better hanging out in the better vacation spots waiting tourist tricks.'[14] However, in her 1981 book *Ordeal*, the born-again Linda graphically recounts how she *was* prostituted by Traynor, whom she portrays as a vicious, deranged pimp before hitting the 'big-time'. At the same time, she does confirm that she would always liked to have been a 'proper' movie star.[15]

Harrowing as her story is, it is apparently not typical of feature-length hardcore. Other actresses, such as Annette Haven, have testified before Grand Juries in defence of the hardcore industry, and thus far there have been no other stories like Linda's. There are more disturbing stories emanating from the loop industry, many of whose performers do appear to be prostitutes. Yet it does not appear that loops offer particularly attractive work to women of that profession. As the producer Mark Rotsler pointed out, film work, which often took up to twelve or sixteen hours a day, paid only $75 a day, while the average prostitute could earn the same in three hours or so.[16]

As the star of *Deep Throat*, Linda Lovelace received $1200 for a week's work. Following her rise to fame, she was contracted for $25,000 in *Deep Throat 2*. This seems to have been the major lure of hardcore. Indeed, the financial incentives were sufficient to entice nationally known models such as Marilyn Chambers and Catherine Burgess. The former is still doing well under the managership of Chuck Traynor through personal appearances, product endorsement for love aids, and so forth.

While actresses like Jacqueline Bisset and Diane Keen came to be embarrassed by subsequent press exposure of their earlier softcore work, hardcore actresses sought to shed the former anonymity of their profession. They gave interviews in men's magazines and did promotional and endorsement work. Such work was of course economically essential to the expansion and mass marketing of hardcore, just as toys and T-shirts were needed to stimulate the renaissance of the Hollywood film industry in the seventies, spearheaded by *Jaws* and *Star Wars*.

It is interesting to note how this celebrity system struck an important chord in its audience. The interviews provide reassurance that the actresses concerned are not prostitutes, and so actually *enjoy* their work.

In men's magazines such as *Club International* regular features such as 'Celebrity Indiscretions' titillated the reader with the revelation that many popular female personalities had at some stage exposed their bodies for sexual appraisal. The better known the personality, the greater the fanfare. One issue of *Club International* carries the editorial caption.

MOST WANTED. Our front runners in the readers' popularity poll for MOST WANTED NUDE! [References to accompanying photographs of Britt Ekland, Blondie, Jaclyn Smith and Anna Ford.] Anna still leads the field, but we're almost being inundated, and Sue Lawley is coming up pretty fast on the rails.[17]

Among these names, we find those of singers and newscasters as well as actresses. The interest for the audience seems to lie in the thought that even 'nice' girls might be ready to oblige. That is to say, any woman a man finds attractive might reciprocate his sexual interest in the way he would like. This is very important to the audience, because it makes them feel secure about their own sexuality.

Hardcore actresses have, of course, already demonstrated in a more obvious way their willingness to play along in this game of reciprocity. And yet the interviews suggest that even more is demanded. Almost every interview eventually leads to the question of whether or not the actress *really* enjoys making certain scenes.

What's it like to do it in front of the camera? . . . Nothing bothers me about it. Because I've been a bikini dancer, I've nude danced. I'm used to walking nude around my farm in Maine, and, you know, sex and nudity has always been just a very natural trip with me.[18]

Such persistent curiosity seems to reveal the viewers' implicit understanding that hardcore is not real but dramatised. What they then want to know is whether the actress is really like her screen self and also whether she 'surrendered' to her role and so broke the barrier between illusion and reality necessitated by the construction of the film.

We shall see that this issue of whether the actress enjoyed her role is of the first importance for the confirmed viewer. For, whilst the erection and ejaculation of the hardcore actor signifies his apparently real arousal, the actress can only signify her pleasure by sound and gesture. Unlike the former, the latter response can be faked. This creates anxiety in the viewer about what real feminine pleasure looks like and then about whether this actress is a good 'faker' or a 'real' sensualist.

The complexity of this issue is further indicated by what has been said earlier about the 'special' kind of actor required for hardcore work. Do the performers concentrate on their work or on some private stimulus? Such questions reveal that sex films are not simply vehicles for 'escapism'. On the contrary, they reveal that these films feed upon the anxieties of their aficionados, who may be described as in some sense 'neurotic' about sexuality.

As sex films of all categories demonstrate, the anxiety focuses primarily on the physical rather than the mental aspects, despite the evidence that, even for men, the usual physiological stimuli are often insufficient to overcome the kind of psychological inhibitions experienced in a studio set-up. Accordingly, films such as *Deep Throat* seek to stimulate performance by example. This may explain why they are insufficiently stimulating to many people – women especially – who would not contemplate sitting through such films. They seem to be more assured that sex is not the compulsive, orgiastic exercise that is presented on the screen.

For those more anxious about physical performance, which men are supposed to be, sex films do serve as instruction. The traditional Christian taboos about sex surely increase curiosity about this aspect. Nevertheless, decensorship did not produce commercially successful sex-instruction films. The sustained market response for sober instructional manuals such as Dr Robert Chartham's *Sex Manners for Men* has proved considerably less than that for fictionalised material.

Perhaps instructional material was too successful in demythologising sexual taboos and so failed to meet the demand of a major market sector for sexual mythologies, old or new. The entertainment industry of the capitalist West found greatest profit in addressing the 'neurotic' consumer. What is so interesting is that the industry chose to do this by adapting 'B' films into skinflicks and loops into feature-length hardcore. In other words, it created *new* products to be viewed in the public cinema and left the loop industry to its own devices.

This was a commercially risky enterprise. Whatever the gains to be made, feature-length sex films demanded vastly increased budgets (as compared with loops), plus heavy expenditure on marketing and distribution. Why did the industry not adopt the expedient chosen by some small cinemas, of showing a medley of loops? These could more than satisfy prurient curiosity and could be made in greater quantity for tiny budgets, much as they now are for the home video market.

The reason seems to lie in the dramatic limitations of loops. Loops were traditionally made for a very determined market who would pay law-breakers handsomely. Within this market, the incidence of neurosis seems to have been much higher, as witnessed by the greater number of 'specialist' films showing torture, excretion, sex with animals and so on. These deviances are rarely found in feature-length hardcore. In some measure this is due to self-censorship by its makers. More especially, though, it is due to the demand in the mass market for mass-taste sex. Lesbianism is the only deviance constantly favoured in these films; male homosexuality very occasionally occurs, as in *Joanna*. And, contrary to the impression given by writers such as Andrea Dworkin, rape and female bondage play a very small part in such films.

Indeed, the same goes for the material on display in many sex shops. The Private sex shop in Nottingham is a branch of the largest sex-shop chain in Britain. Twenty-five of its shelves are stocked with pin-up and heterosexual material; four with male gay and transvestite material. Only one shelf carried bondage, with twelve of the magazines concentrating on female domination of males and four on male domination of females. I am not suggesting that this survey proves anything, but it surely does point to an urgent need for statistics with which to test the frequent claim that male violence towards women is the predominant subject matter of sex books and films.

The short running-time of loops means that plot is sacrificed in order to give 'value for money'. This means a concentration on activity, which allows little space for revelation of the characters' motives for doing what they do. Dialogue, where included, is confined to staccato commentary such 'Let's get it on', 'Mmm, suck that nipple', 'Eat my pussy', 'Fuck me harder' and so forth. Occasionally there is a stunningly silly gem such as 'Fuck me with that great horsecock!' In the main though, the soundtrack is a litany of moans and groans dubbed over wobbly supermarket muzak. A lot of this is found in feature-length films as well, although greater efforts are often made to link the dialogue to the action – as for instance in the film *Inspirations*, where a girl being fucked by an Indian guru cries to him, 'Fill me with your holy Hindu come!' The most one can say about this gem is that it does appear to have been *scripted*!

Another common feature is the close-up of genitalia in action, often reminiscent of films of open-heart surgery. Yet the most striking of these formulaic devices is the 'come shot', where the man ejaculates on the face or breasts of the woman. This is invariably a cue for her to smear herself in the semen, taste it, swallow it and so forth. To the uninitiated viewer this is rather shocking. Ejaculation usually takes place inside the woman; to withdraw at such a crucial instant seems actually a denial of pleasure. Also there cannot be too many women who enjoy smearing themselves with semen and tasting it.

In fact, the *raison d'être* of the come shot is to provide evidence of the actor's real pleasure, whilst the actress's manipulation of the semen is witness to her endorsement of masculine fulfilment. As a dramatic device this therefore functions in the same way as the moaning and writhing typical of such films. Yet, for the reasons mentioned earlier, the visual evidence for female pleasure is never as convincing as for male. In fact the come shot subverts the whole exercise because it emphasises this difference. It is the endeavour to overcome this difference which helps explain the emergence of feature-length films.

Extension of the running-time offers greater scope to represent motivation through plot and characterisation. The absurdities of plotting can also be reduced, and, correspondingly, the allegories of liberation and so forth can be more effectively reinforced. However, it must be said that these opportunities were rarely taken up in sex films of the seventies. Instead, the makers relied intuitively on the proven appeal of popular entertainment. Thus they were happy to build up the celebrity status of their casts, hoping in time-honoured fashion to make audience identification with the characters more easy, and so reducing the need to develop characterisation. They seem to have had little interest in wrestling with the subtleties of dramatisation, unlike, say, Bertolucci in *Last Tango in Paris*. The new sexploitation industry was not developed to take risks: it could not afford to with its modest budgets, short shooting schedules and inexperienced staff.

One common way in which a solution to this problem was sought was by reworking familiar popular films. *Double Indemnity* was retailored to become *Eruption*; *All about Eve* was reworked as *The Budding of Brie*; *Nine 'til Five* became *Eight 'til Four*; and so on. Then there were a plethora of spoofs, such as *Flesh Gordon*, *The Other Cinderella*, *Dracula Erotica* and *The Erotic Adventures of Zorro*. And, as we would expect, literary classics such as *Fanny Hill* and *The Story of O* were made into films.

The adaptation of these familiar themes represented yet another attempt to breach the barrier set up in loops between illusion and reality. By feeding an established fiction the films in question sought to establish dramatic empathy with their audiences. The fact that most failed miserably in this respect seems to be due to their tendency to masculinise their female characters. This strategy requires the realism of the plot to be sacrificed to the improbable drives of the characters. Their uncontrollable sexuality shatters coherent plots into anarchic episodes.

For instance, in *Nine 'til Five* the complications of the plot stem from the realistic efforts of the principal heroines to challenge the male hierarchy of a typical office. Yet, in the hardcore derivative *Eight 'til Four*, the heroines are so masculinised in their sexual appetite that the viewer can take it for granted that every character is at some stage going to indulge her sexual desire. In real life, the viewer often feels a similar compulsion, which is the seed of his neurosis. In mirroring his satyr-like desires, *Eight 'til Four* combines all its characters in a variety of sexual trysts which break the model plot into episodes and create a sexual utopia.

In this fantasy world, practical considerations such as time, place, status, contraception, children, impotence and disease present no obstacle to ecstatic sexual activity. Here lies the potential menace of the viewer's cravings. Were they to be realised as in *Eight 'til Four*, then the efficient operation of the office would collapse into a perpetual anarchy where the female boss was collectively screwed by her underlings, where the photocopier served as a pedestal on which to fuck filing clerks, and so forth. No society could conduct its daily business on this basis. The viewer knows this, and can participate only through masturbation rather than orgy. He is active only in the context of a never-never world like Arcadia, the home of the satyr.

Like his twentieth-century counterpart, the mythological satyr embodied the anarchy that results from sexual licence. In numerous paintings we see the rural idyll of Arcadia interrupted by his forays. In a Greek red-figure dish of about 500 BC by the Brygos painter, we see that even the ordering figure of the chief goddess Hera has to be defended from satyrs by the combined might of Hermes and Heracles.

Nevertheless, the Greeks and Romans did celebrate the spirit of abandonment represented by these followers of Bacchus. Indeed, classical mythology warns of the perils of denying the power of this spirit. In legend, King Pentheus is a rational, responsible monarch who seeks to prohibit what he sees as the excesses of the exclusively female Bacchae, who include a number of his own close relatives. In doing this, Pentheus sets himself against their god, Bacchus, and so becomes guilty of the highest of crimes – 'hubris'. The god punishes him by enticing him to view the rites of the Bacchae, which men are forbidden to do. There he is spotted by his mother and aunts, who in their abandoned frenzy mistake him for a lion and tear him to pieces.

This story horrified later Christian commentators such as Abbé Banier, writing in the seventeenth century. His antipathy to pagan worship seems to have made this legend almost unintelligible to him:

> The Greeks having received that feast [Bacchic rites] . . . added to it several particular ceremonies and, amongst them, some very infamous ones which always shocked such persons as had any remains of Modesty or Shame. These feasts were very often suppressed by public Authority, but licentiousness and lewdness always found means to re-establish them. Ladies of Great Distinction, princesses and even queens, were initiated in those mysteries, from which Chastity and Modesty were entirely banished. We cannot read the first apologists for Christianity, without approving the manner in which they have reproached the pagans on this subject. . . .[19]

This confrontation between the two religious traditions highlights aspects which are of paramount significance in sex films. The Abbé is shocked not simply by the indecency of these rites, but also by the fact that all the participants were female – 'those foolish distracted women', as he calls them a few lines later. What he calls 'distraction' these women called *ekstasis*, meaning a state of physical and mental abandonment which they believed to be a gift of Bacchus. We, of course, still use the word 'ecstasy' to describe a state such as sexual bliss.

In classical culture, the secrets of attaining Bacchic ecstasy were known only to women, whose success in maintaining secrecy leaves us unable to interpret the famous murals in the House of the Mysteries in Pompeii. We have seen that the mystery of female ecstasy is the predominant theme of feature-length sex films. We have also seen that, no matter how hard these films try, they cannot reveal the mystery by any technical or dramatic device. There are of course no means by which men can transcend their subjective and biological differences in order to experience female ecstasy. Yet they might hope that a film could offer them a surrogate experience through something like dramatic 'catharsis'.

In the days of strict censorship, views like the Abbé Banier's forbade drama to attempt such a thing openly. Decensorship made the attempt possible, but economic considerations subverted it, as 'liberation' through the dramatic medium of film became a mass-marketable product. In the capitalist West such consumables are usually disposable due to in-built obsolescence. The curiosity of the male consumer to 'see' female ecstasy recorded on film provided a recognisable demand which was, by a stroke of irony, impossible to satisfy simply by filming sexual performance. Thus, the repetitious showing of sex in hardcore films constitutes a kind of in-built obsolescence for the viewer. By failing to deliver what it promises, this means of 'revelation' keeps the neurotic viewer coming back for more in film after film. Accordingly the former taboo guilt of the typical viewer is sublimated into a guilt about why he suffers the tedium of a third-rate artistic product in order to allay his neurosis about female reciprocation of his urges.

We have seen that the dramatic devices such as masculinisation or exaggerated orgasms which are employed to improve the effects of filmed sex serve only to remind the viewer how different male and female pleasure are. Indeed, most men already know this from their own sexual experience. They know that they do not express their sexual pleasure as demonstratively or for as long as women can. On the contrary, a man learns, or is taught, that, in order to avoid being a selfish lover, he must often distance himself from the sex act. His biological capacity to be satisfied more quickly and finally is a liability for which he must compensate by concentrating upon his performance. Sex manuals make this abundantly clear:

Unless the man can master his progress toward orgasm, successful lovemaking still runs a high risk. This control is not easy to achieve, but every man is capable of it and he should never give up until he has achieved it . . . he can reach orgasm within two to five minutes of his penis becoming erect. The normal woman, unless she is of a very highly passionate nature, requires at least fifteen minutes to travel the same distance . . . while you are stimulating your wife and being stimulated by her, every now and again distract your concentration from what you are doing and what is being done to you by thinking about something quite divorced from lovemaking.[20]

The question of what goals (if any) a man seeks in performing sex well is beyond the scope of this paper. What feature-length sex films have to tell us is that men seem to turn to them for relief from their anxieties about attaining sexual satisfaction. The device of masculinisation in particular seems to recognise the viewer's wish for his desires to be reciprocated – for *mutal* satisfaction. Yet, ironically, the more the woman abandons herself like a man, the less likely are men to find in sex films the mutuality they anxiously seek. The viewer's frustration inevitably has something to do with the dramatic difficulty of revealing the secrets of female pleasure, but it also felicitously suits the interests of both the entertainment industry and the establishment. There is much to be said for the common notion that the crassness of sex films reflects the maladies of the society that produced them.

NOTES

1. Bernard Williams *et al.*, *Report of the Committee on Obscenity and Film Censorship*, House of Commons Command Paper no. 7772 (1979), Appendix.
2. Kate Millett, *Sexual Politics* (London: Hart-Davis, 1970).
3. Andrea Dworkin, *Pornography: Men Possessing Women* (London: Women's Press, 1981) p. 66.
4. See for example Elizabeth Wilson, *What is to be Done about Violence against Women?* (Harmondsworth: Penguin, 1983).
5. Dworkin, *Pornography*, p. 199.
6. Morse Peckham, *Art and Pornography* (New York: Basic Books, 1969).
7. See for example Roland Auguet, *The Roman Games* (London: Panther, 1975).
8. Quoted in John Sutherland, *Offensive Literature* (London: Junction Books, 1982) p. 118.

9. 'J', *The Sensuous Woman* (London: Mayflower, 1971) back cover.
10. Linda Lovelace, *Inside Linda Lovelace* (New York: Foursquare Books, 1976) p. 80.
11. *Cinema Blue*, no. 10 (Apr 1977) 47.
12. 'J', *The Sensuous Woman*, pp. 78–9.
13. Lovelace, *Inside Linda Lovelace*, p. 81.
14. Ibid.
15. Linda Lovelace, *Ordeal* (London: W. H. Allen, 1981) p. 202.
16. *Fiesta Late Night Video*, 1, no. 1, 35–9.
17. *Club International*, 8, no. 12.
18. Barbara Bourbon, interviewed in *Cinema Blue*, no. 1 (Summer 1976) 60.
19. Abbé Banier, commentary on Ovid's *Metamorphoses* (Amsterdam, 1732; repr. New York: Garland, 1976) Explication to fables 8, 9, 10 of book III.
20. Robert Chartham, *Sex Manners for Men* (London: New English Library, 1967) pp. 101–3.

Part Two
Theoretical

5

Is the Gaze Feminist?
Pornography, Film and Feminism

MAGGIE HUMM

It is often claimed nowadays that we have entered a period of feminist criticism even if there are many debates over what techniques are actually feminist. Yet there is no area in which feminist criticism has been formulated so theoretically, and has dominated so conclusively, as in the realm of contemporary film writing. Since 1975, when Laura Mulvey and others first linked sexual representation in film with an implied male voyeur, feminist theories about the 'gaze' have acquired the weight of orthodoxy in film criticism. To fail to use gaze theory as a critical starting-point is to be devalued as a serious film critic. Of course, the issue is not only about how particular film techniques are constructed in a submissive/dominant diegesis but also about their cumulative effect on women and men in a society now pervaded by the acceptable imagery of soft pornography. But to ask why film critics, feminist or otherwise, deconstruct patriarchal controls in cinema only in terms of the gaze is to raise an important issue for film criticism concerning the interrelationship of pornography, criticism and feminism. I want to trace the ideas of feminist film critics and thereby assess their claims – not the least problematic is that the gaze is the only means of patriarchal expression in cinema.

Feminist sociologists working within the broad area of sexual theory have established that male spectators watching films link themselves as subjects constituted in signification with their own sexual desires – between what they see and what they want to be.[1] In response to these findings feminist film critics began to analyse how pleasure comes from identification with dominant–submissive imagery in film and how this is differently received by men and by women.

In 'Is the Gaze Male?' E. Ann Kaplan sums up this evolution in feminist film theory from a sociological to a psychoanalytic approach and gave the theory its most appropriate appellation. But the problem with the concept of the 'gaze' hinges, paradoxically, on feminists' expert attention to representation and the male spectator. Feminist criticism has not, as yet, explored the ways in which the representation of sexuality denies women a sexual *voice* as well as a sexual subjectivity. Film, pornographic or not, is no longer a silent medium. We need to understand the way that both language *and* image combine within film to dominate women.

In order to raise questions about the narrowness of recent feminist film criticism on sexuality and provide some alternatives I intend to juxtapose readings of *Klute* and *Variety* to test the utility of combining linguistic with film criticism. Both films are about the roles of a woman's body *and* her voice within pornography. Before analysing these films, in detail let me deal briefly with the theories which now shape feminist film criticism and also with the difficulty in setting boundaries between pornography, erotic art and mainstream cinema.

It is by now accepted that women are the objects of a male gaze in mainstream cinema. We are excluded from our own 'looks' not only at the level of film technique – in shot–reverse–shot – but also at the level of the narrative. The work of Laura Mulvey and Peter Wollen, both as film-makers and as theorists, and the essays of Annette Kuhn and E. Ann Kaplan offer strategies for identifying and deconstructing a male domination of film imagery. Using psychoanalysis, these critics provide methods for reading film and exposing patriarchal techniques and ideologies. In particular, they have shown how the eroticisation of women on the screen comes about through the way cinema assumes a male spectator and encourages his voyeurism through specific camera and narrative techniques.

The gaze is both a metaphor in film criticism and an integral part of film discourse and narrative. Laura Mulvey first introduced the idea that men looking at women in film use two forms of mastery over her: a sadistic voyeurism which controls women's sexuality through dominating male characters, and a symbolic fetishisation of women's sexuality.[2] Mulvey shows that cinema enables this male gaze to create the illusion, through a complicated system of point-of-view, that the male spectator is producing the gaze. The male character carries the gaze of the male spectator as his assistant. Women are objectified erotic objects existing in film simply as recipients of the male gaze. The aim, then, for Mulvey is to explain the function of film in the erotic violation of women by revealing its system of voyeuristic pleasure. To Mulvey, feminist directors have only to generate new notions of female sexuality by using *avant-garde* practices of spectator–film relationships in order to deconstruct the scopic gaze.

Mulvey's criticism has done a lot to help us examine the question of the gendered spectator; yet, because her method derives from psychoanalytic accounts, via Lacan, of the formation of female subjectivity, it allows little scope for analysing female subjectivity in its semiotic or social discourses. Mulvey sets up too rigid a divide between visual analysis and contextual discourse. In any case, psychoanalysis has not dealt adequately with desire, since it does not read sexuality as that which must be continually produced.

My own teaching has provided a case that illustrates, for me, the impossibility of isolating a technical analysis of camera positions, however sophisticated, from the contextual discourse in which they occur. My Women's Studies class were watching *Not a Love Story* armed with Ruby Rich's attack on the film in *Feminist Review*. Rich argues that the film cannot be feminist since it uses a camera 'gaze' which simulates, through intimate zooms, the vantage point of a typical male customer of pornography. The class largely rejected Rich's reading, not because they disagreed with her technical deconstruction, but because, for them, the film's meaning was lodged in the stories and accounts of the feminist women interviewed as much as in camera movements. A psycho-analytic reading, in other words, did not satisfy these women students. The voices of fascinating and independent women (however problematically presented) won out over the visual construction of spectator relations.[3]

The problem, then, for feminist criticism is not simply that of distinguishing between cinema form and cinema viewer, but also that traditional cinema viewing is not so easily and simply dispensed with. Any attempt simply to deny that viewers are moved by what they hear as well as by what they see will create an imbalance.

So it seemed to me that it should be equally taken for granted that women in cinema are often denied control over their discourse. Feminist linguists, from Robin Lakoff on, have described how men use their everyday speech acts to exclude women from conversational and public space.[4] In cinema the mechanics of that exclusion are more complicated than those of sexual fetishisation and require detailed attention. Of course it could be argued that discourse analysis is inappropriate for pornographic/erotic film, since the image of a female as sex object is so overwhelmingly dominant. But feminist critics have turned to pornography because it *does* offer stereotypes of the inconsistencies and contradictions within dominant traditions of representation. Through feminist analysis of pornography we can more easily identify the absent women in patriarchal discourse and make the cracks and fissures which will enable her to speak. We now understand that the visual representation of women in films by men is never realistic or adequate, since film style encodes a misogynistic perspective. Criticism of pornography/erotic film can thus raise questions for the female spectator about the relation of her image to her life. Since the transformation of female representation points to the speed with which symbolic slippage occurs from film to everyday culture, feminist criticism needs a more complex analysis to understand the meaning and function of sexual imagery.

Yet all contemporary criticism about sexuality and film seems doomed to oscillate between this psychoanalytic heritage and the sociological one where visual imagery *determines* social relations. For example, some anti-pornography campaigns make the mistake of assuming that men imagine female sexuality to be as it is represented by pictures of women in pornographic magazines, films or books and this betrays a fallacious elision of representation and reality.[5]

This position contrasts with the more sophisticated critique of Foucault, who suggests that it is the *language* of sexuality which scripts social positions.[6] I want to combine, then, analysis of film language with analysis of film imagery to propose a stage beyond the spectator/subject of psychoanalytic film theory. I want to place alongside existing critiques of film which describe the interpolation of a gendered subject the analysis of what that subject hears or does not hear.

As we have seen, feminist analysis of spectator identification has concentrated on mainstream cinema, in particular on *film noir*, and within that on shot organisation. Identification is described in terms of the look, and film read as the construction of a series of looks involving the spectator through techniques of shot–reverse–shot. Since point-of-view shots are 30 per cent of all shots in a film there is good evidence to support this critical deconstruction of the apparently 'transparent' cinema. That the cinema is voyeuristic is self-evident. Nor is it surprising that cinematic voyeurism should be for women a problematic mode of identification. But, as I shall suggest in my analysis of *Variety*, many women directors are taking the problematic of voyeurism as the *content* of their own films. If one of the most important areas of feminist criticism is the critique of the 'gaze', an equally crucial aspect of women and cinema, it seems to me, concerns the representation of discourse.

But, if what is at stake is not 'looking' but also 'speaking', we can take feminist analysis a step further by investigating the other side of the dyad – a woman subject's relation to the process of speaking. Much of pornography is a combination of verbal and visual stimulation. One example is *Penthouse* magazine, which uses a letters page, 'Forum', in order to incorporate more explicit sexual imagery than is permitted to its soft-porn photography. Readers' letters describe acts of sex and are often constructed as realistic narrative using more explicit vocabulary ('cock', 'clit' and the like) than can the picture-sequence stories. In one example I examined,[7] many correspondents were exact about age or marital status, even though they may have shared what Angela Carter calls the 'anonymous social world' of pornography in their love of motel settings.[8] If the letters relied on a predictable vocabulary in which penis strokes were always 'deep and furious' or body perfume always 'light', they did have a sensuality denaturalised in the visual imagery of the rest of the magazine. The *actions* of sexuality are markedly absent in *Penthouse*'s picture sequences with the weak innuendo of their sub-titles: 'Her favourite weekend game'; 'Oh, I just adore playing doctors and nurses'; 'She pouts, "Up and at 'em, Rebecca."' There is also a clear relation between soft pornography and the more 'acceptable' artistic representation of sexuality, since *Penthouse* has offered with every subscription a free calendar photographed by Helmut Newton, the house photographer of *Vogue* magazine. This raises the further issue of the utility of defining boundaries between modes of sexual representation.

It would be schematically gratifying to make clear distinctions between *kinds* of pornography – soft porn, hard porn, Hollywood cinema and so forth – and to offer patriarchy separate modes of criticism. It seems to me crucial that the representation of sexuality in mainstream cinema should not be studied apart from other pornography. That way we do not lose ourselves again in what is, or is not, pornographic. Pornography is too easily regarded by liberals and by antagonists as a privileged form of representation.

The excuses of the libertarian sixties are evident in Susan Sontag's seminal essay 'The Pornographic Imagination', which claims not only that pornography has 'peculiar access to some truth' but that it 'can be shared when it projects itself into art'. The security of a 'cultured' spectator continues through Morse Peckham's *Art and Pornography* into Andrea Dworkin's revealing interview with Elizabeth Wilson, where she speaks of her early interest in 'high class intellectual pornography'.[9]

Yet the larger cultural terrain of which both feminist theory and the cinema it describes are representative is the 'media society', the period said to have begun sometime in the late fifties, and variously labelled the 'age of televison' or the 'society of the spectacle'. It is a period marked by pornographic imagery. Feminist film critics are happy to describe this as the 'society of the gaze'. But there are also very real material facts about our society which mark real changes in sexual violence and pornography. The ubiquity of advertising imagery and the hegemony of modes of imagery make it impossible to avoid being desensitised to an imagery of violence and therefore the manipulation of even intimate sexuality. What this means is that the possibilities of eroticism and the ways we want to be sexual beings are determined by forces outside our control. To counter this development feminist film critics offer us the subversion of the gaze. What I shall argue, however, is that the theoretical claims for this approach are inadequate no matter how the term 'pornography' is defined. It is not only that the approach is narrow but also that there are other, larger ways in which it cannot address the sexual politics of contemporary cinema. These ways have to do most of all with the symbolisation of sexuality, both verbal *and* visual, throughout the terrain of representation. They make it possible to handle the specificity and complexity of sexual forms. They suggest that there is no privileged form of representation, since sexual fiction, pornography and mainstream cinema employ similar verbal modes, symbolic codes and genre conventions. Many pornographic scenarios in fiction project compensatory images whose dominant theme is exhibitionism and anonymity.[10] Much of mainstream cinema projects the self-same images.

Klute is a film in which the coded gaze imposes itself with particular force, through a continuous series of camera oppositions and strategic points of view which identify a (male) spectator with male characters. Directed by Alan Pakula in 1971, it is one of a cycle of such films, including *Dressed to Kill* and *Looking for Mr Goodbar*, which show women being hunted down and physically assaulted. The narrative of *Klute* is the gradual exposing of Bree Daniel's career of prostitution by Klute, an ex-policeman hired by Cable (finally revealed as the psychopathic killer) to solve a mutual friend's murder. The real work of *Klute*, as of most *films noir*, is to show, step by step, how men are free to violate those women placed outside conventional family life, and finally incorporate them into a heterosexual monogamous sterility where control is possible.

Using a series of narrative oppositions between Bree's own investigation, in psychoanalysis, into her sexuality, and Klute's increasing sexual control over Bree through *his* investigation, the film homogenises camera movements with patriarchal ideology. The opening shot focuses on Klute sitting centrally at a family meal using his gaze like a horizontal camera pan, so that his character is our ingress to the film's narrative. The murderer, like Klute, is allowed the freedom of sweeping horizontals as he masturbates, to Bree's recorded voice, sitting at a similarly long boardroom table. Pakula himself has pointed out that he intended the film to enclose women in a series of narrow verticals, of camera 'tunnels', or fragment them in doorways in opposition to the masculine horizontal.[11]

Not surprisingly, critical response to *Klute* revolves around the question of the gaze. Whether critics adopt an iconographic, a structuralist or semiotic approach, most have felt compelled to read the film only on a diegetic level of the physical/perceptual control of female sexuality. Christine Gledhill notes that the thriller is dedicated to destroying a woman's 'threat to male control of the world'. Terry Lovell from the different direction of iconography draws attention to the gendered relation of protagonist and spectator.[12] Thus it seems that *Klute* can be read only for its visual encoding of signifiers – that the presumed statement, *énoncé*, of the film equates a visual dimunition of Bree with her diminished sexuality.

It is possible, *à la* Lovell, to read *Klute* iconographically, watching Bree's own city sexuality, signified by her hippy clothing, submit to the moral authority Klute brings with him from the opening country scene. A semiological examination would involve other oppositions all equally visual. Bree's attempt to gain independent sexuality through a modelling career is correlated with deformity, since the models are inspected under masks of burnt faces. With his key to Bree's apartment Klute changes Bree's feminine colour 'keys' of purple and red to a masculine blue and grey. Structurally, the film displaces Bree's recounting of her childhood in the warm setting of wall-mounted photographs of children with her increasing child-like need for Klute.

The problem that then faces us is that to ascribe a function to Bree's speaking voice might easily be to appropriate for it a text characterised by other critics as relying only on scenic *visual* codes. But the film's more complex exposition of male misogyny is produced primarily through the *juxtaposition* of voice with *mise-en-scène*. The film is equally concerned to establish how males exclude Bree from speaking as they simultaneously exclude her from her own sexuality. *Klute* resorts to a number of devices to signify male opposition to female speech and sight. One of these devices is the verbal opposition of Bree's 'story' scenes, which develop chronologically (but not, of course, heuristically), to provide an authorial sub-code within the other codes of the film. The psychiatric interviews are the prime examples of this device. In the first interview Bree, if not confident, gives an intelligent, even witty account of her behaviour and *mores* as a prostitute. Knowing more than her clients, she can deliberately control their sexuality by creating any appropriate sexual narrative. The scene is supported by one dramatising her call-girl success. Together the two scenes locate prostitution in its social context with a revealing attention to the necessary and attractive detail of Bree's everyday body preparation. Bree, as female subject, refuses to *hear* herself from the place of patriarchy, and can insist instead on a disjunction between her self-image and that projected for her in the 'discourse' of prostitution.

This paradigm of an independent speech of sexuality cannot be sustained. Bree has another interview with her psychiatrist after Klute begins to objectify and control Bree's career. In the second interview Bree speaks less coherently and, in particular, cannot now recount, or account for, the physical sensations of prostitution. The sound-track is merely a sequence of distancing sub-titles which replace former sexual similes. The film's attention to Bree's voice as the foundation of Klute's investigation is further evidence of a male fear of feminine discourse. The tape of Bree speaking out her self-created sexual therapy is stolen by Cable and held by Klute. Both are using Bree's voice to stimulate themselves, as it were, rather than returning the voice to its subject. The stealing of Bree's voice is duplicated by the theft of another tape of prostitute sexuality recording the orgasmic killing of Bree's friend Arlene.

In other words, in these cases the tape recorded, like the camera in others, is *the* apparatus which controls, manipulates and objectifies women. The *sound* of Arlene's murder is used to distance Bree, i.e. to oppress her through the *discourse* of murder itself. Through depriving Bree of access to her own language of sexuality Klute is able, finally, to relegate her to a suburban patriarchy. He takes exception to Bree's last telephoned encounter as he has already stripped her apartment bare of visual imagery. The intimate stories of sex which Bree creates for her clients – for example, the fascinating account of Italian aristocratic sexuality – are dislodged and rendered inoperative just as she was unable to perform St Joan (with *her* voices) with Klute as spectator.

The mutilated female voice is a vital character in *Klute*. Together with the camera it gives currency to a narrative of male violence. *Klute* has a clear semantic sub-code to be placed alongside the codes of the visual. The film cannot be reduced to the level of its visual signifiers alone, since we must say that its complexity is best understood through combining the two approaches of 'discourse' and 'gaze'. It is these two codes together that produce a thematics of voyeurism and rape. In fact, if Pakula had wished us only to *see* Bree's mutilation he would have made a very different film. I would argue that *Klute* horrifies female spectators not just because we are 'framed' in Bree's journey from prostitution to monogamous suburbia but also because we *hear* her sexuality repressed and murdered.

The question to address is: how can a feminist film address or construct a female listener while giving her a female gaze? How can female desire be inscribed within viewing and listening practices? Speaking of *Variety* in 'The Pleasure in Looking', the director Bette Gordon says that one of the problems from a feminist perspective is that the 'pleasure of looking in the cinema has been connected with the centrality of the image of the female figure'. She suggests that one of her central projects in *Variety* is to raise 'various questions: How does the camera produce and construct certain prescribed positions and marginalise others'.[13] The film shows that the voice has a particular stake in the reconstitution of a more diverse female sexuality. As we have seen from the controversy over *Not a Love Story*, feminists are suspicious of films about pornography because they must, necessarily, utilise pornographic images. *Variety* tries to escape the dilemma by showing that representations of female sexuality need different semantic as well as visual codes. Indeed there is no *visual* representation in the film of the central character, Christine, *having* sex. Gordon fulfils Angela Carter's wish for a moral pornographer who would use pornography as a critique of current relations between the sexes.[14] Like *Klute*, *Variety* consciously structures two codes into its text, setting up a power struggle between the saying and the selling of sexuality. Through her generation of a double perspective, Gordon ensures that the active spectator will question pornographic representation.

Gordon's choice of pornography as subject is not haphazard. She is relying on the cinematic training of her audience. She knows that audiences are now knowledgeable about the formulae of thrillers, *film noir* and blue movies and uses the genre of the classic *film noir* to draw us into her story. By replacing a male with a female investigator she ensures that attributes of the *noir* genre, in particular the central character's function as the only source of morality, will shift to the female. Christine wants to be a writer, a coiner of words, but instead coins money working as a ticket-taker in a pornographic movie house. Her boyfriend is an investigative reporter trying to establish Mafia involvement in a local fish market. However, it is Christine who 'tells' the story of that connection through trailing a client of the theatre to the market and his other business assignments. Further, Christine articulates elaborate stories of sexuality, recounting her reaction to the pornography she sees (which we never see in full but only *overhear*); and collects fresh fantasies of imaginary sexual encounters. Her voice is juxtaposed with the face of her love, now mute and angry from his felt inadequacy.

So Gordon is trying to evoke and dismiss the visual manipulation of female sexuality by balancing it with the effect of speech. Pornography offers Gordon a vantage point for analysing sexual paradigms. Through Christine's stories we sense the negative presence of what else could be, but isn't being, said or shown. As Shklovsky says, we can 'make strange' a genre, which Gordon does by avoiding a certain logical resolution to her thriller, since both female protagonist and male victim slip away from the final frame.

Of course, like *Klute*, *Variety* is concerned with the visual in several different ways. However, Gordon denies her viewers the satisfaction of a male voyeur by creating a fresh female voyeur through Christine's obsessive tracking of her anonymous client. Christine watches men playing baseball and reading porn, and watches herself being seduced by her client in a fantasy sequence. Gordon works continually to turn around our expectations of feminine representation. In the opening sequence Christine dresses alongside a girlfriend, using the cameras as *her* mirror. Mirrors are not the narcissistic Lacanian nightmare they are in, say, *The Eyes of Laura Mars* but a means for Christine actively to understand how she is female. *She* controls the camera gaze, making men uncomfortable in the porn shop, or opening and closing curtains in the motel to delimit our gaze of the victim, who, in any case, never *sees* his pursuer. Gordon jokes continually about 'looks'. Christine promises to 'look out' for her client's favourite porn film as if it was an everyday TV programme; she arrives at the ball game to hear only a snatch of the Anthem 'Look, can you see by the dawn's fading light'; she parodies blue movies by wearing a blue sweater and a blue waspie and enjoys the traditional iconography of *film noir* flicking away her cigarette under the only street lamp.

Gordon wants us to attend to the visual but also wants us to be conscious of its alternative. Her strategy encourages a dual consciousness, an active questioning of the typical 'way of seeing' female sexuality. It is the voice which stresses the shift in a realignment of the traditional genre. The insertion of verbal fantasy challenges the notion of a sexuality fixed by the visual and Gordon forces us into the gap between verbal fantasy and visual identity.

Bette Gordon uses the tape recorder as a means for introducing this split subjectivity into her film. In her apartment Christine listens to her answering machine, continually switching it on and off and replaying significant moments. The voices are those of her mother, her boyfriend and a dirty phone caller. They are disembodied traces of social life which do not mesh with Christine's own activity in control of the machine and her dominating speeches elsewhere in the film. Our cues to her emotions and the ideas and feelings of other actors are always located semantically. The fantasy stories (which are written by the novelist Kathy Acker) are a kind of Hitchhiker's Guide to a Sexual Galaxy and spoken in a deliberately unrealistic and discontinuous way. To begin with, the voice is monotonous, contrasting markedly with a standardised thriller. Christine incorporates long pauses, and stresses *connectives* – for example, 'to' – rather than nouns. They become what Luce Irigaray calls an italicised version of what passes for the neutral – a way of evoking and dismissing the usual male pornographic narrative of violent sex. Gordon's is a significant linguistic statement about the inappropriate matching of female voice and female image in mainstream cinema. She interrupts the dominant *film noir* mode to suggest a more unstable female sexuality.

The most consistent aural device that Gordon uses is perhaps her most important statement about the *process* of female speech. In one scene call-girls, waitresses and out-of-work actresses meet with Christine in a bar, enjoying their stories of prostitution. They encourage each other to talk and share subversive strategies. The stories are funny but engage us as much through the intimate connection Gordon makes between content (verbal catalogues of male aggression) and social context (the spoken detail of daily finances or fetishisms). The message is simply but convincing. Only women together can *speak* porn in order subjectively/objectively to analyse their sexuality. Gordon's depiction of prostitution focuses not on the violent sexual relation of male client and female victim but rather on the experience and behaviour of the women who perform responses to their own performances. Where Mulvey speaks of the fetishised image of female sexuality freezing the male look, Gordon uses an erotic voice to freeze the male gaze.

We have found a number of devices in which Gordon plays her film images off against her film discourse, encouraging us to question our possible experience of her subject. Gordon refuses an image of female sexuality as the site of male violence in order to generate a more complex picture of sexuality. As Juliet Mitchell suggests in *Psychoanalysis and Feminism*, sexuality is like a langauge only brought into being through the process of learning.

The question we should pose is not 'What is pornography?' but the question E. Ann Kaplan poses in *Women in Film Noir*: 'What is being said about women here?' and (more appositely) 'Who is speaking?' It is important, therefore, not to isolate particular modes of representation but to look at the *context* of representation which includes the voice in a fuller discourse of sexuality. Only thus can we see the extent of cinematic misogyny visual *and* verbal – particularly if, as Deleuze has argued, 'one only desires as a function of an assemblage where one is enclosed'.[15] For to be the *object* of desire is always to be defined in the passive voice. Yet, from Scheherezade on, women have always known how to utilise the power of speech to save their sexuality. The axiomatic conjunction of spectator and desire reduces our readings and serves consequently to limit our interventions within representation – interventions which might harbour alternative sexualities for feminism. Part of the problem of dealing with speech in film has no doubt to do with a domination of explicit sexual imagery. But it is articulation which must be stressed, not simply representation. The emphasis thus shifts from using films of sexuality as evidence of explicit sexism to an examination of how sexism operates within a fuller regime of representation. The eye of the beholder has been under a feminist optometrics but his ear has escaped attention.

This essay has offered some tentative counter-arguments about the cinematic apparatus of sexual enunciation and, within that, on the place of women's imagery and discourse. No analysis can provide a solution to the mechanisms by which men exclude women from playing an active part in narratives, but we can attempt to engage with this better, I think, by regarding film as a series of interconnected visual *and* verbal discourses. For what is at stake is a final break in the collaboration between the male gaze and male speech in the exercise of male power.

NOTES

1. In an extensive survey of 668 respondents answering a 42-item questionnaire Pauline Bart provides convincing evidence that the imagery of pornography desensitises males not only to sexual violence but also to pornography itself. See 'The Difference Worlds of Women and Men: Attitudes toward Pornography and Reponses to *Not a Love Story* – a Film about Pornography', *Women's Studies International Forum*, VIII, no. 4 (1985) 307–22.
2. See Laura Mulvey, 'Visual Pleasure and Narrative Cinema', *Screen*, XVI, no. 3 (1975). In a recent article Mulvey has modified her position to give a much more sophisticated account of the gaze. See *History Workshop Journal*, no. 23 (Spring 1987) 2–19.
3. *Not a Love Story* is a documentary account of pornography directed by Bonnie Klein. It has been the focus of several feminist critiques, attacking the privileging of heterosexuality among other issues. Ruby Rich's article is 'Anti-Porn: Soft Issue, Hard World', *Feminist Review*, no. 13 (Feb 1983).
4. See the overview of this research by Dale Spender in *Man Made Language* (London: Routledge and Kegan Paul, 1980).

5. There is a very good account of the anti-pornography campaigns in C. Vance (ed.), *Pleasure and Desire* (London: Routledge and Kegan Paul, 1984).
6. See in particular the concluding chapter of Michel Foucault, *The History of Sexuality*, vol. I (New York: Vintage Books, 1980).
7. 'Forum', *Penthouse*, xx, no. 7 (July 1985).
8. Angela Carter, *The Sadeian Woman* (London: Virago, 1979).
9. See Susan Sontag, 'The Pornographic Imagination', in *Styles of Radical Will* (New York: Farrar, Straus and Giroux, 1966) p. 232; Morse Peckham, *Art and Pornography* (New York: Basic Books, 1969); 'Interview with Andrea Dworkin', *Feminist Review*, no. 11 (June 1982).
10. See M. Charney, *Sexual Fiction* (London: Methuen, 1981).
11. Quoted in E. Ann Kaplan (ed.), *Women in Film Noir* (London: British Film Institute, 1978).
12. See Christine Gledhill, '*Klute* I: a Contemporary Film Noir and Feminist Criticism', in *Women in Film Noir*; Terry Lovell, *Pictures of Reality: Aesthetics, Politics and Pleasure* (London: British Film Institute, 1980).
13. Both Gordon quotes from Bette Gordon, '*Variety*: the Pleasure in Looking', in Vance, *Pleasure and Desire*, p. 191.
14. Carter, *The Sadeian Woman*, pp. 19–20.
15. Quoted in P. Foss and M. Morris (eds), *Language, Sexuality and Subversion* (Darlington, NSW: Feral Press, 1978).

6

Looking at Women
Notes Toward a Theory of Porn

GARY DAY

In recent years there has been much discussion of pornography by feminists, who have stressed that, while pornography is one of the most obvious forms of violence against women, it should not be studied in isolation from the way women are presented generally in capitalist society. The image of women in pornography, so the argument goes, is continuous with their portrayal in the mass media as a whole. There too women are presented as objects, creatures subordinate to the male will, and pornography is the culmination of this process. It is, many feminists have claimed, a form of rape, celebrating male power. While there is some truth in this analysis, its implication that, because all women are portrayed as objects, all images of women are therefore pornographic does rather oversimplify the relationship between pornography and other representations. To say that a television commercial in which Edna O'Brien advertises the *Guardian* is on a par with a sexually explicit film is plainly absurd. Pornography, though it may have something in common with the representation of women in general, also has its own autonomy, working in different ways with different effects from, say, *Woman's Own*, one obvious difference being that each addresses a different type of audience.

Pornography is notoriously difficult to define and the problem is complicated by its availability in written, photographic and cinematic forms, to say nothing of its various genres and subgenres. Lesley Stern, writing on the subject, can only come to an 'Inconclusion',[1] while Mariana Valverde notes, somewhat ruefully, that 'the problem is that there are no litmus tests for what is or is not pornography'.[2] Feminist criticism which has glossed over the complexities of pornography has found itself in an embarrassing and wholly unlooked-for alliance with the moralists of the New Right, who urge women to return to their traditional role of wife and mother. Of course, this is exactly the sort of thing that feminism is trying to resist, but the effects of patriarchal discourse (in which feminists conduct their debate) are such that they find themselves manoeuvred into a position of either/or: either they are for the family and against pornography or they are for pornography and against the family.

One problem, then, is not only how to conceive pornography but also how to think or theorise about women within a discourse that only allows women to be thought or theorised in a certain way. Patriarchal discourse constructs woman as 'other': she is different because she is not male; and one consequence of this is that she is not credited with that unified subjectivity so beloved of male capitalist culture. Instead she is offered a series of contradictory positions: virgin, whore, nurturer, destroyer, glamour girl, old cow. Woman in patriarchal society exists in fragments which, interestingly enough, is the idiom of hardcore pornography, where the parts are greater than the whole.

As patriarchal discourse is the only available discourse for women, they inevitably, in questioning their positions and analysing their status, reproduce the contradictions of that discourse in their attempt to overthrow it. Thus feminist views of pornography present women as victims, which links with the way in which patriarchy defines women as passive. Moreover, if feminism then goes on to say that women should take control of their destiny, it allies itself, again unwittingly, with the values of independence, control and action, all of which are masculine values underpinning an economic system which holds women in subjection. Thus, although feminists object to the way in which women are represented in capitalist society, they nevertheless support it by ratifying one set of representations at the same time as they are trying to dismantle another. Given, therefore, the difficulties of constructing an image of women outside the available discourses, together with feminism's rejection of the way women are represented in those discourses, women must be postulated as an absence – an idea developed by Luce Irigaray, who argues that, because Western discourse has excluded woman, she exists only in terms of an essence which has not yet been recognised. This essence, she continues, is centred on woman's body, which Irigaray discusses as a multiplicity of desires. But this approach, in attempting to differentiate male and female sexuality, nevertheless supports patriarchy's view of woman as *primarily* a sexual being.[3] Perhaps a great part of the problem could be removed if the word 'woman' were replaced by the plural 'women', a useful distinction made by Monique Wittig, who writes that 'Our first task . . . is to dissociate "women" (the class within which we fight) and "woman", the myth. For "woman" . . . is only an imaginary formation, while "women" is the product of a social relationship.'[4] According to this view, then, as long as the word 'woman' retains its mythic status, the human female will always be a myth, a mystery, a non-being, an absence.

Patriarchal discourse constructs women not as they want to be but as men want them to be, and in this sense they are absent to themselves but present to men. Another way of expressing this is to say that women are objects of desire rather than desiring subjects. The reason for this, Lacan says, is that the 'I' position is not so readily available to girls as it is to boys. He claims that the child enters language – or what Lacan calls the symbolic order – as a result of his or her separation from the mother and simultaneous identification with the father, the representative of culture in the family. Little girls, however, although they experience the same separation from their mothers as little boys, do not identify with the father, because they lack the phallus which is the condition for identification with him. Thus, for Lacan, men have a monopoly of the 'I' position, while women, not possessing the phallus, occupy a negative position in language. There is only one way for women to enter the symbolic sphere and that is for them to internalise male desire, to see themselves as men see them. This view would certainly help to undermine those defenders of porn who say that women enter into it of their own free will, for it suggests that this free will is nothing other than an absolute conformity to male desire, a willingness to be what men desire them to be in order to win male approval.

But, if Lacanian theory can account for feminine absence, it does so at the cost of a contradiction, for, since entry into the symbolic is dependent on a lack – the separation of mother and child – that lack is the very basis of language, making it difficult to talk about its positive and negative terms. Moreover, it seems that, because masculine desire dominates speech, this lack is most acutely felt by males, whose position in language is supposed to give them more authority and self-possession than women have. Perhaps the final irony is that Lacan sees male desire as positing woman as the fulfilment of the lack caused by separation from the mother. Thus it seems that man, not woman, is the absence, since he needs her to complete him, though it has to be stressed that this still gives woman a secondary role.

Despite its drawbacks, however, or perhaps because of them, Lacan's theory does draw attention to the fact that, if woman is absent to herself, she is also absent to men; or, more particularly, what is really absent is the mother for whom every other woman is a substitute: as each substitute is revealed as such, the man passes on to the next, in the hope that she will be the real mother, though she never is. In this respect, women are like signs – they stand for what is not there. The appetite for more and more women is clearly depicted in hardcore pornography, where again the women are expendable. What hardcore pornography also shows is the frustration which lies at the heart of this appetite and it is apparent in the crude and frenzied way in which the sex act, is performed, particularly by the men. The women involved are possessed as themselves or as bodies but not as what they represent or signify, and it is the frustration arising from this which perhaps causes the aggression towards and objectification of women that one finds in pornography.

But what of the female desire? Many feminists have deplored the lack of a female erotica and have argued that criticising pornography is not enough – attention must also be given to 'constructing and exploring diverse sexualities for feminism'.[5] Such a move may have to take into account the work of the radical biologist Mary Jane Sherfey, who notes that 'a woman could go on having orgasms indefinitely if physical exhaustion did not intervene'.[6] This view of women's sexuality also defines her as absence, but here her absence lies in her excess, which cannot be contained by such patriarchal forms as monogamy. Sherfey's ideas show the feminine to be something that goes beyond, to be a principle of disorder threatening the coherence of bourgeois culture. Indeed, Sherfey goes so far as to say that it was necessary to suppress female sexuality in order that civilisation as we know it could evolve.

There are a number of things wrong with Sherfey's account, the most obvious being that her definition of woman is biological and so does not take sufficient account of how she is socially constructed. Furthermore, her account of female appetite can too readily be assimilated to the categories of nymphomania and aggression, thus confining it within the limits of patriarchy which she is trying to transcend. Nevertheless, Sherfey's account of female desire is an improvement on the pallid romantic heroine dutifully waiting for the right man, which even today is still offered as a role model to many young girls.

In the discourse of patriarchy, then, woman emerges as absent and contradictory and she is also a sign or a substitute for the original lost object. It is important to bear these ideas in mind when discussing pornography, because, although pornography generates an image of woman, it does so on the basis of how she already appears in society. If woman is an absence, a blank screen, then it is easy for men to project their fantasies onto her and so she becomes what they wish. In this way she acts as a signifier of male desire, but in so far as she is the object of that desire she is also its signified; she is at once both signifier and signified and this gives her a closure and completeness which makes her impenetrable. The whole process is aggravated by her being 'possessed', but not as what she represents.

This view involves looking at the formal features of porn and only the briefest possible start can be made here. Such an investigation seems to me long overdue, for current definitions of porn are plainly inadequate. To say, for example, that porn is violence against women is only partly true, for there is a lot of pornography where women are depicted as the aggressors forcing men into having sex with them. Furthermore, the violence-against-women view does not account for gay pornography, which involves no women and yet is still pornography. Pornography, in fact, is such a prodigious topic that it is impossible to settle on any one definition that will apply to the whole of it. Most definitions of pornography only accurately describe a part of it, which, bearing in mind how pornography deals precisely in parts, is strangely apt. Indeed, trying to answer the question 'What is pornography?' is rather like trying to answer the question 'What is literature?' for, as Terry Eagleton has pointed out, most theories of literature 'unconsciously "foreground" a particular literary genre and derive their general pronouncements frrom this'.[7] The word 'unconsciously' suggests that criticism is not unmotivated in its classifications, so, if it operates like this on literature, how much greater will be its motivation when analysing pornography? For, in however crude a way, pornography deals with sexuality, the repression of which helps constitute the unconscious in the first place.

Most definitions of pornography are the result of looking at the material as if it is what it appears to be, and there is little attempt to make a distinction between depth and surface. But what is shown in a pornographic picture is not the same as what the picture means. The subject matter of pornography is sexuality, which, since it has a complicated biological development interacting at all times with social forces, and is the source and object of a great deal of fantasy, cannot be dealt with in any straightforward manner. Sexuality is both a product and a process and partakes of so many elements that it is never obvious, though that is exactly what pornography tries to make it. Moreover, pornography is a regime of representation and as such is not simply a reflection of how, for example, women are portrayed outside pornography; rather it is a construction of an uncomplicated sexuality, though in the process it unwittingly says a lot of other things about sexuality. Pornography, especially in its visual forms, tries to say something about sex with sex: signifier and signified seem fused in a relationship of pure presence and it is this which makes the meaning of pornography seem so obvious. However, as has been shown, the meaning of pornography is far from obvious and closer examination reveals that sex operates only as a signifier, while what is signified remains unclear. This perhaps reverses Freud's classic view, which, put simply, sees everything as capable of representing sex, as if that were the basis, the irreducible reality, the signified of all signifiers. Now, however, sex itself becomes a signifier – a signifier, moreover, which is in excess of any signified. Of course there are signifieds in pornography, but what these are depends on the interpretative strategies one brings to bear on them.

For Annette Kuhn, the project of pornography is to

construct sexual difference . . . by defining it in terms of, even reducing it to, bodily parts marked culturally, and/or within the context of the image as feminine. [Its] conviction is that sexuality equals femininity: [its] promise [is] that femininity may be investigated, even understood, by scrutinising its visible marks.[8]

According to this argument, then, pornography signifies femininity, which it constructs purely in bodily terms. However, as pornography does this repeatedly, there is a suggestion that it does not know the object it constructs and its boring repetitions come to signify this frustration. Indeed, there is a strong case to be made here that what the female body signifies is not femininity but male desire, in so far as it is presented as aggressive and insatiable, qualities normally associated with men. Thus the sense of failure and frustration generated by pornography is not the result of not knowing the other but rather the consequence of the male recognising neither himself nor his desire. The female body, far from being the signified, becomes the signifier of maleness, while the male, in wanting to know about femininity, only misrecognises himself. The fact that the signified becomes the signifier not only shows the excess of the latter over the former; it also suggests the inability of patriarchal discourse to imagine anything other than itself. In pornography, the voyeur sees himself made strange.

The depiction of desire in pornography is a complicated affair, because of the nature of desire. Neither a mere urge nor simply the product of a conscious intention, desire resists representation. Moreover, as Jeffrey Weeks has noted, desire is not 'a relationship to a real object but is a relationship to phantasy',[9] which means that any attempt to picture desire is an attempt to articulate a relationship between representation and non-representation. Further factors which inhibit the representation of desire are, according to Weeks, the fact that it is both historical and ahistorical.[10] Finally, ever since Freud, desire has been seen as that which is disruptive, as exceeding the forms which give it some measure of expression. Pornography, however, glosses over the complexities of desire, robbing it of its radical potential. In celebrating male power over women, for example, it serves the interests of the social order in which it appears, despite the fact that that social order marginalises it.

Since we live in a patriarchal society, pornography presents desire from the male point of view. At a very basic level, this involves looking at the naked female form, most readily available in the pin-ups which are found in softcore magazines. It is difficult to account for this compulsion to stare at a woman without clothes. Perhaps it is necessary to see the other in order to experience a sense of self, or perhaps it is a question of wanting to know, and therefore control, what is different. Whatever the reasons, the desire is not a new one. Before the pin-up there was the nude in art, and the difference between the two lies in the fact that the latter's pose was such that she barely seemed conscious of her sexuality, while the former most certainly is. More specifically, she is conscious of her power to arouse the spectator with what Annette

Kuhn calls the 'come on' look.[11] This does not mean that the voyeur's ownership of the female form, which he has bought and which he possesses through the look, is lost, but it does indicate, in however small a way, that he is being challenged. In effect, what he is being presented with through the 'come on' is the fact that he does not own the female body as he would like. The 'come on' is the model's consciousness of her sexuality and its power to arouse the voyeur, and it is also a sign that she is the owner of her body and that her display of it is a display of ownership. It is probably this display of ownership which makes the man want to own the model's body, something he cannot do, but has the illusion of doing because he can make the model respond to his fantasies. In reality, though, she is not possessed, and it is that knowledge which lends an independence to her gaze as she stares at the camera. Her not actually being possessed is also apparent in so far as there is no man in the picture with her, and this ultimately suggests that she has no need of the voyeur though he has need of her. He is redundant, and the irony for patriarchy is that the femininity it constructs as being safe and knowable, because it is simply a body, turns out to be a threat and to leave no room for maleness at all.

Of course, none of this alters the fact that society is so constructed that males have the power to make women appear in these magazines, or that, in posing, they are objectified. But what goes on behind the scenes is not the same as, nor should it blind us to, what is happening in the pictures themselves. The models may be presented for male consumption, but their apparent availability is dependent on certain conditions which, when examined closely, ultimately question the very idea of their availability. Even if this be accepted, it may be objected that the models have internalised male desire and, although they may be in control, are nevertheless presenting themselves as males would like to see them. While this is no doubt true it is also equally true that the effects of internalisation are not predictable and do not always work in the male's best interest, since the pictures are capable of constructing him as superfluous. A more fruitful criticism along these lines might be to concentrate on how the voyeur's look is somehow necessary to define the model as female – though, reciprocally, the voyeur also needs to see the model's body in order to define himself as male. It would be interesting to consider why the voyeur needs the model's body, and not her gaze, so to define himself.

In many pin-ups the model is shown with her hand hovering over her genital region. This can be interpreted in two ways: first, to prevent penetration, and, second, as masturbation. In the first case the non-availability of the model is again underlined, but the second case goes further and suggests her sexual self-sufficiency: not only is she not available but she also has no need of men. Furthermore, her auto-erotic pleasure, if such it be, mirrors the man's auto-erotic pleasure as he looks at her. Her image thus becomes a reflection of his own activity and indicates that gazing at a pin-up is analogous to Narcissus captivated by his own image in the pool. Once more the voyeur does not recognise himself. As for the model, she, lacking an identity of her own, can only ape the voyeur she cannot see.

It is difficult to know why men obtain enjoyment from pin-ups when these same pin-ups seem to be repudiating them. Perhaps some sort of masochism is at work here, for the voyeur's relationship to the pin-up variety of pornography could be described as taking pleasure in what he hasn't got: he desires what he can never possess and it is within this matrix that he experiences his enjoyment. Perhaps this can be developed further, for what the pin-up, in allowing the voyeur to fantasise about her without actually possessing her, is actually doing is providing an outlet for his desire for the mother which was repressed at the resolution of the Oedipus complex. In other words, the model acts as a substitute for the mother and allows the voyeur symbolically to enjoy what he was originally denied. Seen in this light the absence of the male in the pin-up takes on a new meaning, for if he were there then his presence would block the fulfilment of the incestuous fantasy, whereas his absence facilitates it.

To see the pin-up as a substitute mother supports Weeks's point about desire having fantasy as its object, and it also goes some way towards explaining both one aspect of softcore pornography and one criticism of pornography generally. The first point concerns those magazines which are devoted exclusively to big-breasted women. As the breast is the infant's first source of nourishment it represents nurturing and motherhood, and it therefore seems fair to say that the models in these magazines are more overt mother figures than the ordinary pin-ups. We also see in these specialist magazines the beginning of a process that culminates in the broken bodies of hardcore pornography. In the 'busty' magazines the breasts are the exclusive objects of concern, and this perception of

parts of the body, rather than of the body as a whole, is characteristic
of that stage of infancy which Lacan refers to as the 'imaginary',
where there is no sense of a unified self but rather a free-flow
situation in which objects merge with and replace one another in
a closed circuit. The infant here experiences himself or herself in
terms of various conflicting forces, drives and instincts.

This leads on to the second point, the criticism that men who
look at pornography are childish. If looking at pin-ups is really a
release for the incestuous fantasy, then pornography is indeed
childish, for it deals with infantile desires and, as seen above,
infantile perceptions. Another aspect of pornography which shows
its infantile character is that in it the pleasure principle reigns
supreme, the reality principle does not apply and so sex always
takes place almost entirely without context or motivation.

If the pin-up is the mother figure she is also the 'whore', for her
picture, being mass-produced, is available to anyone who may
care to look at it. Perhaps the combination of these two 'characters'
explains why some pornography shows women being mistreated.
Where this happens, it is possible to argue that the model is
being punished for being a faithless mother. Alternatively, the
punishment could be seen as an attempt to control the mother and
guard against any disappointment which might result if she were
allowed to regulate the voyeur's needs, as she did in infancy. In
short, the punishment is a compensatory control over a substitute
mother for not being able to control the real one when it mattered.
This control, however, is not just manifest in the mistreatment of
women. More fundamentally, it is there in the way the model, as
blank space, is made to have male desires. Thus in desiring the
model the voyeur, whether he is looking at soft or hardcore
pornography, is desiring his own desire, which suggests that he
is in some sense alienated from it. Male desire is alienated in the
model, who as a signifier of male desire is herself alienated from
her femininity. Pornography may present sex as immediate and
unproblematic but a close reading of pornographic images shows
that the participants are alienated from their sexuality. By being
made to have male desires females are, in an act analogous to
castration, robbed of their sexuality. This act also serves to punish
them for those early maternal betrayals and to bring their mythical
rapacious sexuality, which men have feared for centuries, under
control. The irony of all this for pornography is that female
sexuality, which it ostensibly shows, parades and displays, is in

fact the very thing that pornography represses. What it instead reveals is male desire desiring to be desired by male desire. Pornography thus has a narcissistic quality – the voyeur is simply looking in a mirror to confirm his desire – and the ubiquity of male desire indicates that beneath the heterosexual surface there may be a homosexual core. Lastly, the above account suggests that pornography is not about desiring but about being desired. The voyeur is less a desiring subject that someone who wants to be desired and everything in the pornographic scenario is designed to bring about this effect. However, it is difficult to identify the person who is doing the desiring, for it is both the voyeur and model, or substitute mother, onto whom he has projected his desire.

One of the most off-putting aspects of the pin-up is, in Annette Kuhn's phrase, the 'split beaver'.[12] In such pictures, the subject is reduced to one part of her anatomy. It is offered as the single, irreducible signifier of sexual difference, but, since it appears in isolation from the rest of the body, its impact is that of a meaningless piece of flesh. It is displayed as if for inspection, as though it were something that is hard to believe. The starkness of it reassures the voyeur that it is what it is and no other thing, yet it has no identity. Perhaps one reason for the voyeur's fascination with this object is that it satisfies him that someone else has suffered castration and not he. Another maybe that, as a sign of difference, the female sexual organs can never be fully comprehended within patriarchal discourse and so they remain a mystery to which the voyeur is irresistibly drawn. Indeed, patriarchal discourse's failure to comprehend and integrate the feminine could explain why the female sexual parts are presented in a thing-like way. Lacking a proper identity, within the terms allowed by patriarchy, they constantly have to be identified; hence their continuous reappearance.

The 'thingness' of the female sexual organs, as presented by these magazines, is a threat to the ideas of character, subjectivity and humanity as understood in patriarchal discourse, and yet, strangely, male patriarchal subjects persist in seeking out this thingness (perhaps to affirm their own non-thingness?). As long as it is on the outside it remains a threat, and so its constant appearance may be an attempt to bring it into the inside. However, once experienced there, it is found to be unworthy and so is cast out again in a movement which reaffirms that culture is about values, not things. Culture is thus established by expelling female sexuality, which may explain why open displays of it only exist at the margins of culture, in pornography and the like.

Two final points on pin-ups remain to be made. The first is that their relationship with the voyeur caricatures the philosopher's search for truth. In Western societies truth is something that has lain behind appearances and must be uncovered; just as the philosopher wants to uncover truth, so the voyeur wants to uncover women. Truth and sexuality are thus linked as they indeed were in Genesis, when after eating the fruit of the tree of knowledge Adam and Eve knew each other's nakedness. This connection between truth and sexuality needs further exploration. The second point is that the pin-up sexualises the environment in which she appears. A woman in front of a fireplace gives the fireplace sexual connotations, while a women who is in a dining room gives a double meaning to the word 'eating'. In other words, it is possible to see in the pin-up's power to transform her surroundings a return of the myth of the female's devouring sexuality. If, however, the model is really a signifier of male desire, then this myth properly refers to male, not female, sexuality.

Another popular staple of softcore porn is lesbianism. Photographs of lesbian erotic play seem to promise the voyeur – because, like all photos, they purport to record and not to interpret – that they will teach him not only about the female body but also about female sexual behaviour. In actual fact, however, they teach him neither: first, because the models are arranged to please the voyeur, not to instruct him; and, secondly, because the women in the pictures relate to each other not as women, but as men. With their paraphernalia of dildos and vibrators they relate to each other's bodies as a man would relate to a female body, and with the usual props of stockings and make-up their appeal to each other is the appeal of a woman to a man. Thus, although on the surface the male appears to be absent from these pictures, he is included not just because the pictures are directed to him but also because of the woman's total behaviour towards each other. Moreover, since, in part anyway, each woman relates to the other in a male-like way, the voyeur can easily identify with their behaviour.

This identification, however, is a complex affair, for not only is the male identifying with male behaviour as expressed through a female body, but, in wanting to be desired, he is also, by extension, identifying with each woman's desire to be desired, i.e. as a woman is by a man; the voyeur identifies with both male and female aspects of the picture. What is happening here is that the sexual difference on which pornography insists is losing its clarity. Such trans-sexual identification continues the process of fragmentation and disunity which begins with the pin-ups, where only parts of the female body are presented, not the whole.

The desire for the mother which is part of softcore pornography is also to be found in hardcore pornography, particularly in the loop. The hardcore loops seems all-inclusive, except, perhaps, of the spectator, a point to which I shall return. It can contain both humans and animals, and, on the evidence of what I have seen, I should not be surprised if, somewhere in the world, loops were produced with reptiles and even insects included in the cast. The typical scenario of the hardcore loop is of a woman who either initiates sex or is easily persuaded into it because 'it's what she really wants', and it ends with her licking the semen that the man has ejaculated over her. The man and the woman can, of course, be multiplied, and in a significant number of loops the participants show, through their dialogue, an awareness of their audience. Sex is presented as perverse and forbidden. Indeed, to watch one of these loops is to be convinced of the accuracy of Freud's phrase 'polymorphous perversity', which he used to describe infantile sexuality. I have already suggested that pornography, in part at least, represents a regression to the desires of infancy, and the perversity which is the *sine qua non* of pornography would support this. The body and all its functions and even the setting in which the act takes place are, in the loop, completely appropriated for sexual purposes. This can be interpreted as an assertion of power, both by men and by women, to subdue and adapt their environment to their own sexual ends. The forbidden character of sex in these loops emerges in the way that intercourse takes place among people between whom it would not normally or conventionally take place. Thus the bride has sex with everyone except her husband; there are numerous adulteries and even examples of incest. To do what is forbidden is an expression of power, the individual defying the right of the community to determine what is and is not acceptable behaviour for him or her.

Assertions of power link the forbidden character of sex in pornography with the way the environment is appropriated for sexual purposes, and the forbidden is also part and parcel of the perversity of pornography, for to be perverse is to persist in something that should not be done. Also, just as the perversity of pornography evokes infancy, so does the forbidden, for it is during infancy that that weightiest of all commands is laid on the little boy: 'Thou shalt not sleep with thy mother.' Furthermore, it might be argued that the power to transform the environment is reminiscent of that infantile omnipotence, the sense that young child has of everything existing for its convenience. There is one further way in which pornography depicts an infantile state. It is, says Steven Marcus, a world of 'abundance and sexual plentitude',[13] a world of fusion where 'Persons . . . are transformed into literal objects; [and] these objects finally coalesce into one object – oneself.'[14] This account of the pornographic world is very close to Lacan's conception of the imaginary, which is also a world of plentitude, without any lacks or exclusions. In it, the infant exists in an immediate, dual relationship with its mother that is eventually broken by the intervention of the father. The existence of forbidden desires together with the dual and fusional world of the loop suggests that what is happening in hardcore pornography is, in part at least, the symbolic realisation of the incestuous fantasy: and it is at this point that the voyeur becomes important.

The voyeur's relationship to softcore is essentially passive, though he can identify with elements of the picture if he so wishes. But in hardcore, where men are present, the urge to identify with what is going on is much greater. The protagonists, in a large number of loops, seem aware of this and actively encourage the identification, but only to block it. Both protagonists comment on how they expect the voyeur wishes he could be involved in the action, but at the same time the woman excludes him by making preferential comments about the man she is with while the man makes disparaging remarks about those who watch but can't do. The risibility of such dialogue does not detract from the fact that it is intended to defy and challenge the voyeur. In fact, the voyeur seems central to the hardcore loops, for what he witnesses is an act whose character is determined by the tension between his participation and his exclusion. Both the act and the protagonists' consciousness of it are constituted by the knowledge that they are being watched by someone who cannot join in. The voyeur is an essential third party who is defined and challenged and in whose defeat and discomfort the protagonists revel. Now, if the hardcore loop is partially about the realisation of the incestuous fantasy, the voyeur in such films seems, from the above account, to be cast in the role of the father. However, in this re-enactment of the Oedipal drama the father is excluded and the forbidden desire triumphs.

To say that the hardcore loop is partially about the realisation of the incestuous fantasy begs the question of who exactly is doing the fantasising – the voyeur or the protagonists? The answer, I think, is neither; rather the realisation is inherent in the fusional world of forbidden desires and in the loop's relation with its audience. The realisation of the Oedipal fantasy, in other words, is not so much a question of individuals as a question of structure.

The Oedipus complex is not just a family drama but also a social one, for when the child accepts the father's prohibition he is, in effect, acknowledging the right of others to say what he can and cannot do and as such he can be said to enter society. He accepts his designated position and the law from society's representative, the father. It therefore follows that, if the hardcore loop is partially about the realisation of the incestuous fantasy, then it is also a refusal to enter society. This might explain why pornography flourishes only at the edge of society and why, when it appears to encroach towards the centre, it is cast out. Society, as it were, plays the father to pornography as pornography plays the son to society. Society's representative *vis à vis* pornography is the voyeur, whom pornography needs to defy and exclude if it is to define its desires as forbidden. Without the voyeur, pornography could not exist; with him, it can refuse to exist in society.

To pass through the Oedipus complex is not just to enter society but also to enter what Lacan calls the 'symbolic order' or language. Language, according to Lacan, symbolises what has been lost when the child emerges from the Oedipus complex. This is the mother's body and his relationship to it. Unlike the imaginary, the symbolic is structured around differences and is characterised by absence and exclusion – the child must accept his sexual difference from the mother, the absence of her body and his exclusion from it. In her place he has language, but this can never replace his desire or the object of that desire, both of which have been repressed. Instead he has a substitute desire, based on an identification with the father – the desire is to occupy the father's position – but this can only ever be symbolic, because it will never give him access to what he has lost. Although this is massive oversimplification of Lacan's theory I hope it brings out the point of language as a symbol of what is no longer present. The application of this theory to hardcore pornography is complex. However, it may explain why pornography, as a medium, resists verbalisation in favour of pictures, for the voyeur's relationship with a photograph at least gives the illusion of being more immediate and direct than his relationship with words. The former suggests that the image, because it is experienced more directly by the voyeur, is continuous with the imaginary where the infant is fused with his mother, thus giving further support to the idea that, at least in the hardcore loop, forbidden desires triumph. There is a problem however, for the imaginary, as a place of fusion and duality, has no space for symbolisaton and yet pornography does, to a certain extent, symbolise the realisation of the incestuous fantasy. How can the imaginary mode of pornography also function symbolically? This shows that great care is needed when discussing pornography in terms of fantasy fulfilment.

Although there are undoubtedly problems in seeing pornography, whether softcore or hardcore, as a refusal to pass through the Oedipus complex, it does perhaps help to explain why, beyond the obvious reasons, pornography alienates feminists. The Oedipal drama is basically a male one and its appearance in pornography eliminates even the potential for a female erotica. Furthermore, to see pornography as a refusal to pass through the Oedipus complex is to draw attention to the way it refuses sexual difference. As Jeffrey Weeks has noted, 'the resolution of the Oedipal crisis is . . . to structure a recognition of sexual difference as necessary for cultural order'.[15] Not to solve the Oedipal crisis is, then, not to accept or acknowledge sexual difference, and this is indeed apparent in pornography by the absence of female sexuality. Thus pornography does not construct sexual differences: it simply makes everything a sign of male sexuality; as in the imaginary, there is no recognition of the other. This is important if one considers Dorothy Dinnerstein's ideas about male development. She says that, because the boy is first attracted to his mother, he must define himself as separate from her in order to achieve a sense of himself as male.[16] In pornography, however, maleness and male desire have, since women are masculinised, nothing to define themselves against; they therefore exist in a vacuum. Without the difference of female desire, pornography can neither present nor confirm male desire, which is its unconscious aim.

This failure at the heart of porn may account for the repetitions and frustrations which seem inherent in it. What the typical hardcore loop concentrates on is the process of sex rather than its beginning or end, and this lack of closure seems ideally suited to a form which deals with male desire without properly identifying it. Indeed, the absence of female sexuality means, in pornography, that male desire is a desire without an object, a signifier in search of a signified, always in excess – ostensibly directed at the other, but in reality trying to signify itself.

Sexual difference is negated not only by the models' being made to signify maleness through their behaviour and through the wearing of penis substitutes but also by men being feminised – for example, by wearing women's clothing or being sodomised by a woman with a dildo. A further way in which sexual difference is neutralised is by presenting the body in pieces. This breaking-up of the body is the fleshy equivalent of the breaking of convention mentioned earlier, and it signifies the fragmentation of the unified subject, whose sexuality of course forms part of that unity. It is bits of the body which, in the hardcore loop especially, are given prominence, and these bits, whether male or female, are rarely filmed in isolation but are conjoined with their opposites. The resulting impression from this is of a profound dissatisfacton with the human form which realises itself in an urge to dismantle and then reassemble it so that it incorporates both 'male' and 'female' sexualities.

This breakdown of difference helps create the dual, fusional world of porn, particularly of the hardcore loop, but it also prevents it from signifying, for signification depends upon difference. It can signify neither female sexuality, which is its ostensible project, nor male sexuality, which is what, unawares, it actually tries to do. And yet there can be no doubt that porn is trying to say something, for there is an intensity and energy about it which cannot be associated with silence. Whatever it is, porn seems to want the *body* to say it, but the body breaks apart under the strain. This fragmentation of the body, however, is also a sign of porn's dissatisfaction with it, as if the ultimate project of porn was to escape out of or through the body to some bodiless state of otherness. This suggests that the body is ultimately disposable, which is exactly its fate in the darkest, farthermost part of porn, the 'snuff' movies (where sex ends in death).

Whatever porn means, however, cannot be established by simply taking it at face value, tempting though this may be due to the shock value of its images. Porn is both fantasy and reality, but, while feminists have been attentive to the latter aspect, they have not, as a whole, been so sensitive to the former. I do not pretend that what is written here can account for all the manifestations of pornography or its relationship with other representations. What I have tried to do is redress the balance slightly by concentrating on one fantasy as it appears in the pin-up and the loop. What is needed, I think, is a greater focus on the signifying practices of porn as well as on their part in the wider discourses of sexuality and power. Only then will we see the full significance of porn, the better to do battle with it, for, as things stand, it is camouflaged by its obviousness, an enemy that cannot be defeated because it is not seen for what it really is.

NOTES

1. Lesley Stern, 'The Body as Evidence: a Critical Review of *The Pornography Problematic*, in *Screen*, 23, no. 5 (Nov–Dec 1982) 39–60.
2. Mariana Valverde, *Sex, Power and Pleasure* (London: Women's Press, 1985) pp. 124–5.
3. Luce Irigaray, *Ce sexe qui n'en est pas un* (Paris: Editions de Minuit, 1977).
4. Quoted in Ann Rosalind Jones, 'Inscribing Femininity: French Theories of the Feminine', in Gayle Green and Coppelia Kahn (eds), *Making a Difference: Feminist Literary Criticism* (London: Methuen, 1985) p. 90.
5. Stern, in *Screen*, 23, no. 5, p. 60.
6. Mary Jane Sherfey, *The Nature and Evolution of Female Sexuality* (New York: Random House, 1972) p. 135.
7. Terry Eagleton, *Literary Theory: An Introduction* (Oxford: Basil Blackwell, 1983) p. 51.
8. Annette Kuhn, *The Power of the Image: Essays on Representation and Sexuality* (London: Routledge and Kegan Paul, 1985) p. 38.
9. Jeffrey Weeks, *Sexuality and its Discontents: Meanings, Myths and Modern Sexualities* (London: Routledge and Kegan Paul, 1985) p. 132.
10. Ibid., p. 157.
11. Annette Kuhn, *The Power of the Image*, p. 42.
12. Ibid., p. 39.
13. Steven Marcus, *The Other Victorians: A Study of Sexuality and Pornography in Mid-Nineteenth Century England* (New York: Meridian Books, 1964) p. 273.
14. Ibid., p. 277.
15. Weeks, *Sexuality and its Discontents*, p. 143.
16. Dorothy Dinnerstein, *The Mermaid and the Minotaur: Sexual Arrangements and Human Malaise* (New York: Harper and Row, 1976).

7

Romance Fiction
Porn for Women?

ALISON ASSITER

According to the blurb Mills and Boon sends out to aspirant authors, the romance novels published by this British company are read in cultures as different from one another as those of the United Kingdom and Japan. In addition, recent research statistics put forward by Mills and Boon also reveal that, in the United Kingdom at least, 28 per cent of all women, from a variety of backgrounds, and across a wide range of age groups, read romance fiction.[1]

In this essay I shall argue that part of the answer to the question 'Why is romance fiction so popular?' is that it is *porn for women*. And, since, I shall argue, porn reinforces the subordination of women, in reading these works women are contributing to the reproduction of their oppression. Nevertheless, I do not wish to denounce these women as the witless dupes of evil ideology, and it is in support of this last point that I begin this essay with a discussion of porn in general.

In the *Fontana Dictionary of Modern Thought*, porn is defined as 'visual, written or recorded communications designed primarily to arouse sexual excitement in the pornographer, as intended audience, or both . . . those for whom porn is a taboo subject tend to impute pornographic aims to all who break their taboo.' Apart from the circularity in this definition (it refers, in a fashion that is left unexplained, to 'the pornographer'), it places too much emphasis on the *intention* of the designer of the material, and not enough on the material itself and its use by the consumer. Reliable reports suggest that in Britain, before the relaxation of various taboos on sex in the late 1960s and early 1970s, copies of the *National Geographic Magazine* were bought for precisely the purpose for which many men now buy their copy of *Penthouse* or *Playboy*, i.e. as material for masturbatory fantasy.[2] One presumes that the

101

writers/designers of the aforesaid magazine did not intend it to be used for this purpose.

Until very recently, the British law defined porn as 'obscene material . . . tending to deprave or corrupt' those who read or look at it.[3] But, as has been all too evident in the various court cases over the years, this definition is vague, to say the least. How are we to decide what is obscene? What does 'tending to deprave and corrupt' mean, and who is the appropriate audience to test for corruption?

Many feminists would criticise both the above definitions for their failure to recognise that, on the whole, it is men who are the consumers of pornography and women who are depicted – in the films, the pictures and the stories. Perhaps the most extreme of the radical feminists is Andrea Dworkin. In her book *Pornography: Men Possessing Women* Dworkin renders porn 'the graphic depiction of women as vile whores', and she says, 'the word has not changed its meaning' from early times on.[4] Etymologically, she points out, the word derives from the Greek *pornē* (harlot) and *graphē* (writing). I believe that Dworkin is right to bring the role of the women depicted in porn into focus but that she is wrong in her emphasis. There is a wealth of difference, nowadays, between the women displayed on page 3 of the British tabloid the *Sun*, or the women in the films on show in Soho, and those who are forced, out of economic necessity, to sell themselves to men.

The most significant difference between the two is that the women in pornographic literature are invariably represented as enjoying their sexual encounters: thus 'Sybil' in *Penthouse*, says, 'Sex is the most important thing in my life.' In a great deal of porn, because it is 'representation', women can be presented as enjoying sex indiscriminately. Prostitutes, however, who engage in sexual activity out of economic necessity, are unlikely to 'enjoy' more than a fraction of their encounters.

Susan Griffin, in her book *Pornography and Silence*, offers an interesting and subtle analysis of the 'pornographic mind'.[5] Porn arises, she argues, through the mistrust of sexuality as a treacherous and powerful force (presumably she means in contemporary Western culture). According to her, the objectified women in pornographic films and pictures represent the sexuality of the consumer of porn: sexuality is perceived in Western culture as 'the enemy within'. Women, because of their closer proximity to 'nature' than men, are seen as expressive of this sexuality, and men therefore seek to control and conquer them. Porn both represents the attempt by the male to control his sexuality, and simultaneously, and ironically, contributes to making it harder to achieve.

Griffin goes a lot further than producing a definition of porn; in fact she is less interested in that than in producing an account of the formation of the 'pornographic mind'. But, extending and extrapolating from her account, we can both define porn and say in what way it contributes to the continuation of women's subordination.

Porn, I suggest, is the representation of the eroticisation of relations of power between the sexes. In the overwhelming majority of cases what is depicted in films and magazines is women as a commodity for male consumption. The woman, like the slave in Hegel's master-slave dialectic, is represented as wanting nothing so much as to satisfy the desires of the man who gazes at her. He, in turns, treats her as an object whose sole wish is to satisfy his desires. Though fantasy is involved in porn, the likelihood is that, even if the man's desires are only satisfied in fantasy, their being satisfied at all serves to reinforce them. Thus the satisfaction, in fantasy, of the man's desire to treat the woman in this way reinforces the behaviour of men in so treating women. Being objectified – treated as a means – has been a major part of women's oppression in general, in Western culture at least. It links back to the mythical alignment of women with 'nature'.

Thus, what is wrong with porn is that it reinforces men's desire to treat women as 'objects' or at least as a means of satisfying of their desires, and not, to use a Kantian expression, as 'ends in themselves'.[6] Treating people as 'ends in themselves' entails, for Kant, treating them autonomously: treating them as self-legislating and self-determining and not, like slaves, as instruments for the satisfaction of others' ends. In porn, however, the women depicted tend to collude in their treatment as means. Frequently the woman is either represented as being, or actually is, happy to see herself this way – her ends are precisely to allow herself to be treated as a means to the satisfaction of the man's desire.

Mainstream romance fiction, I would argue, is a form of pornography. It is porn in precisely the same sense as *Penthouse* and *Mayfair*, except that it is written from the woman's point of view. There is plenty of evidence that the romances are erotic. Who can doubt it when presented with passages such as these: 'Fire ignited at the hard pressure of his mouth, hungry and demanding' (*Strange Bedfellow*, p. 164);[7] 'Gradually he released her from his crushing embrace, letting his hands move over her body, stroking her back, then her sides' (*On Wings of Night*, p. 23);[8] ' "Like this Satin, is this what you want?" he asked sensuously, letting his fingers slide with exquisite tenderness over the high, firm curve of her breasts, covered only by thin gold material' (*Friends and Lovers*, p. 78).[9]

In some recent Mills and Boon romances, and more frequently in the Silhouette novels, the act of penetration is laid before us, graphically described. More often than not, however, one has to read it in between the lines, or after shutting the book. But what is generally on offer in romances is something else: descriptions of sexual desire and sexual fantasy, rather than their fulfilment. In *On Wings of Night*, for example, the heroine sits in 'scented bathwater, still pondering the potential for love that was between the two of them, knowing that she was spinning daydreams' (p. 118). In addition, sexuality is sometimes metaphorically described. Thus as Anne Snitow suggests, we read 'hard fingers', in one Harlequin romance, as the penis.[10] Besides fantasy and metaphor, there is the sexualising of everyday actions. In the typical Mills and Boon romance, the heroine initially dislikes her hero. Yet, even then, contact between the two is made sensual. Maybe it is a parodied sexuality, but the sexuality is certainly there: 'The second dressing was applied; Max's hands were on her shoulders as he pressed the dressing into place. At the unexpected actions, an odd quiver swept through her' (*The Isle of Rainbows*).[11]

As Anne Snitow says of the Harlequin romances, 'they revitalise daily routines by insisting that a woman combing her hair, a woman reaching up to put a plate on a high shelf (so that her knees show beneath the hem, if only there were a viewer), a woman doing what women do all day, is in a constant state of potential sexuality'.[12] The heroines of Mills and Boon and of the other romances are continually overwhelmed by desire. Their desire, moreover, is just like that of the woman depicted in the pages of *Penthouse*: the heroine is not the initiator; she is responding – 'The assault on her senses took her by surprise, gave her no time to bolster her defences against the need to respond to the invasion of her mouth' (*On Wings of Night*, p. 122). If ever there is lovemaking, she – the heroine – responds to the 'needs' of the hero: ' "What do I want of you?" His voice was thoughtful. "Everything. Everything you have to give, Carol, Witch, my Witch.

Your green eyes bewitch me and I want you"' (*On Wings of Night*, p. 122). Indeed, although the body of the text describes the heroine's fantasy, often, when there is real sexual contact between hero and heroine, the text switches to describing his desire for her: '"I want you, my lovely Jancy," he said deep in his throat' (*Jacintha Point*);[13] or 'He crushed her mouth under his, his tongue darting possessively into her mouth, his body pressing hers back against the seat' (*Friends and Lovers*, p. 58).

And the passivity of the heroine's desire sometimes takes the same form as the desire that the woman in the pages of *Penthouse* is represented as having: the wish to have him desiring her. Even where the conscious feelings of the heroine, as is often the case in the Mills and Boon romances, are hatred, disgust and repulsion, underneath she wants him to want her:

> All she needed to recall now what that he was the man who was forcing her into unwanted loveless marriage to satisfy his injured pride. Not that that was the sole satisfaction he required, she thought, suddenly dry mouthed as she remembered the searing effect of his lips and hands, the little shaken storm of desire he had so effortlessly aroused in her.   (*Counterfeit Bride*)[14]

Indeed, sometimes even more than is the case with *Penthouse* or *Playboy*, the woman is the slave to her man's desire: 'He was the warrior; she his captive' (*On Wings of Night*, p. 122). The man is in control, dominant; the woman gratefully, joyously accepting and submitting: 'She willingly let his lips dominate hers for as long as he choose' (*Strange Bedfellow*, p. 164). He is doing the choosing; she acquiescing. In *Jacintha Point*, Laurel is rendered unconscious by a blow on the head and she loses her memory. Her hero, Diego, subsequently controls who she is. In case anyone thinks that this might be a phenomenon brought in by the relaxation of sexual taboos in the late sixties and early seventies, here is Barbara Cartland, writing in 1961: 'He crushed her to him and his lips found hers. He kissed her brutally with a violence which seemed to force the very life from between her lips' (*The Runaway Star*).[15]

Though romances are written from the woman's point of view, they depict women as wanting nothing so much as to have their man desire them, to have him adore them, and for them to satisfy his wants and needs. In all of these respects, the heroine is just like the woman in the pages of *Penthouse* or *Playboy*. Germaine

Greer, in *The Female Eunuch*, argued that there is a gap between 'real porn' and romance.[16] Real porn, she suggests, gets rid of romance. And Beatrix Faust, in *Women, Sex and Porn*, tells us that most women have no interest in porn.[17] She means *Playboy* and *Hustler*. But why should a woman read *Playboy*? If she is heterosexual, why should a picture of a woman be exciting to her? If she is lesbian, she is likely to be put off by the captions, which are obviously intended for a male audience. Why should a women either desire or identify with the women depicted in the fashion of the permanently sexually aroused women in the pages of men-only magazines? Romance heroines are, in many respects, like real women: much of their lives is spent engaged in ordinary pursuits – ordinary for large numbers of women, cross-culturally – such as washing up, or dressing, or combing their hair. The reader needs to be able to see the heroines as in some respects like her or she will have no basis for the identification. A pin-up 'girl' on page 3 of the *Sun* can be represented by her as odd, somewhat immoral, as in no way like herself. The heroine of a Mills and Boon romance, on the other hand, might well be she herself. The romances portray eroticism as legitimate, as part and parcel of everyday life. *Penthouse* represents it as slightly deviant, as outside the scope of most women.

For similar reasons, porn for women could not, as some feminists have suggested it might, involve a reversal of the customary male/female roles. Though there are cases where this happens, fantasising 'crushing' a man under her would be, for most women, too risqué, too immoral, too far removed from her experience. But, just because Mills-and-Boon-type fiction is romantic, it does not follow that it is not pornographic.

Such novels are pornographic, not because they encourage women to play the part of the hustler or the dude, or because they suggest an image of the female covertly taking a peek at her book under her bedclothes. They are pornographic because they paint a picture of the woman wanting nothing so much as to be desired; they present an image of the woman as passive, responding, just like the woman in the pages of *Penthouse* and *Playboy*.

More recently, a feminist has argued that, contrary to my previous argument, many women do respond positively to violent porn. Marion Bower suggests, in fact, that the responses of both men and women to porn are similar, and, that this fact can be explained in psychoanalytic terms.[18] Following the post-Freudian psychoanalyst Melanie Klein, Bower argues that the baby – boy or girl – has both sadistic and masochistic instincts from very early on. This is because it experiences the mother both as a 'good' object that satisfies its desires and as a 'bad' object that frustrates them. It therefore responds to the mother in both sadistic and masochistic ways. Responding positively to violent porn, Bower argues, can be explained in terms of the way both women and men re-enact and possibly even attempt to exorcise many of these early fantasies.

It remains the case, however, that women read far more romantic fiction than violent porn. And, as far as the psychoanalytic explanation goes, there are significant differences in the early experiences of boys and girls. Boys have to differentiate themselves from someone – the mother — who is, in the significant respect, very different from them.[19] The person, by contrast, from whom the girl differentiates herself is, in the significant respect, the same as she. The girl, therefore, in a way, continues to be the mother. A man's sexual fantasies, therefore, can unambiguously re-create his relationship to his mother; he can represent his lover as being solely concerned with the satisfaction of his needs, as his mother was. The woman's fantasy lover, however, will be both mother and father, since, in the psychoanalytic reading, she is, in part, the mother. She is, in fantasy, both child being adored by her mother, and mother desiring father. The romance hero can be represented as possessing qualities of both father and mother: he adores the heroine, like her mother, and yet he is also, like her father, the powerful patriarch.

Thus, while Bower's analysis may account for the responses of some women to violent porn, I do not believe that it either presents a true description of the porn that the majority of women find exciting, or provides the most plausible psychoanalytic explanation of adult sexual fantasies.

Part of the explanation for the popularity of romantic fiction is that the novels are erotic. But they are erotic without going too far from the everyday. They allow women to imagine, as they wash the dishes or make the beds, that they are sexually attractive and desirable. They reinforce fantasies about tall, dark handsome men coming to carry them off. For most women, to fantasise becoming a hustler or a stud would be unreal. Romantic fantasies are sufficiently exciting, because of their play upon erotic imaginings, but also close enough to the experience of many a woman for her not to rule them out as beyond the bounds of possibility.

The readers of romantic fiction and the heroines of the novels are acting out the best parts of the role of the typical woman today, the woman who is often objectified, treated as a symbol, a pin-up. The models in women's magazines encourage women to objectify themselves – to slim, to 'dress up' for their men, to worry about the way they look for others. In 'objectifying' women, the magazines are continuing a long tradition of thought about them: the ancient Greeks imagined women to be closer to nature than men; their role in reproduction connected them to nature's fertility. Rousseau partly idealised and partly denigrated the 'closer to nature' aspect of the female.

Romantic fiction continues this tradition. Thus, in reading it, women are reproducing their oppression. Yet, the reader should not be condemned. Without alternative outlets for their fantasies, it is not surprising that women look to the Mills and Boon genre. Only changes outside the pages of fiction will lead them to a true realisation of their imperfectly represented desires.

NOTES

1. Peter de Mann, 'The Romantic Novel', unpublished paper presented to the Institute of Contemporary Arts (conference on romantic literature, November 1983).
2. A. Moye, 'Pornography', in A. Metcalf and M. Humphries (eds), *The Sexuality of Men* (London: Pluto Press, 1985) p. 53.
3. Bernard Williams *et al.*, *Report of the Committee on Obscenity and Film Censorship*, House of Commons Command Paper no. 772 (1979).
4. Andrea Dworkin, *Pornography: Men Possessing Women* (London: Women's Press, 1982) p. 200.
5. Susan Griffin, *Pornography and Silence* (London: Women's Press, 1981).
6. H. J. Paton, *The Moral Law: Kant's Groundwork of the Metaphysics of Morals* (London: Hutchinson, 1948).
7. J. Dailey, *Strange Bedfellow* (London: Mills and Boon, 1979). Page references in text.
8. C. Conrad, *On Wings of Night* (London: Silhouette Desire, Silhouette Books, 1983). Page references in text.
9. D. Palmer, *Friends and Lovers* (London: Silhouette Desire, Silhouette Books, 1983). Page references in text.
10. A. Snitow, 'Mass Market Romance: Porn for Women is Different', *Radical History Review*, no. 20 (1979).
11. A. Hampson, *The Isle of Rainbows* (London: Mills and Boon, 1978) p. 37.

12. Snitow, in *Radical History Review*, no. 20, p. 145.
13. E. Graham, *Jacintha Point* (London: Mills and Boon, 1980) p. 187.
14. S. Graven, *Counterfeit Bride* (London: Mills and Boon, 1982) p. 196.
15. Barbara Cartland, *The Runaway Star* (London: Pan Books, 1961) p. 105.
16. Germaine Greer, *The Female Eunuch* (New York: McGraw-Hill, 1971).
17. Beatrix Faust, *Women, Sex and Porn* (Harmondsworth: Penguin, 1982).
18. Marion Bower: 'Daring to Speak its Name: the Relation of Women to Pornography', *Feminist Review*, no. 24 (Autumn 1986).
19. See, for instance, Wendy Holloway, 'Heterosexual Sex: Power and Desire for the Other', in S. Cartledge and L. J. Ryan (eds), *Sex and Love* (London: Women's Press, 1983).

Part Three
Critical

8

Beyond Ideology
Kate Millett and the Case for Henry Miller

MICHAEL WOOLF

> *Fundamentally he intended to undermine, if possible, the whole structure of the Puritan ethos which would open the way for correct loving, real loving and consequently art; sensuality, sensibility go hand in hand.*
>
> Lawrence Durrell[1]

> *When he deals with sex he seems to me to achieve a crudity unsurpassed except by the graffiti on the walls of public urinals. . . . In my view,* Tropic of Cancer *is obscene in the simplest sense.*
>
> Walter Allen[2]

No writer has caused greater controversy in the twentieth century than Henry Miller. For Lawrence Durrell, Miller is an inspiration. Norman Mailer sees within him a paradox out of which artistic genius is formed: 'It is as if Henry Miller contains the unadvertised mystery of how much of a monster a great writer must be.'[3]

There are, though, many alternative notions. Walter Allen's sense of a pornographic crudity in Miller's fiction is echoed by Richard Hoggart, who says that Miller's men 'are alone even when they are fornicating'.[4] Kenneth Rexroth relegates Miller's work to the status of naughty-boy scribbling: 'Most of the sexual encounters in *The Tropics* and *The Rosy Crucifixion* are comic accidents, as impersonal as a pratfall. The woman never emerges at all. He characteristically writes of his wives as bad boys talk of their schoolteachers.'[5]

However, the most sustained assault on Miller has come from feminist critics, especially Kate Millett in *Sexual Politics*. She argues

113

that his work expresses a 'neurotic hostility'[6] towards women, 'the yearning to effect a complete depersonalisation';[7] in his prose 'Miller simply converts woman to "cunt" – thing, commodity, matter.'[8] Yet at the same time there is an oblique admiration in Millett's view that Miller offers 'a compendium of sexual neuroses, and his value lies not in freeing us from such afflictions, but in having the honesty to express and dramatise them'.[9]

At the heart of Millett's view is an ideological rejection of Miller's representation of women. There is, though, a sense of distance between ideology and art in Millett's writing. Politics and creativity are seen as strangely separate areas of consciousness that make vastly different kinds of demands. Millett is torn between a political and ideological alienation from Miller's work, and a responsiveness to his creative method and artistic vision. In this respect, her autobiographical work dramatises the supremacy of art over ideology.

In *Sita* and *Flying* she reveals a profound sympathy for many of Miller's attitudes and narrative strategies.[10] Essentially, *Flying* owes much to *Tropic of Cancer* in both method and ideas.[11] Both books occupy a place in the study of the relationship between sex and introspection in American culture. They belong within a tradition of fiction that uses sexual action to assert an anti-Puritan position, and that further sees sexuality as a means of liberating an essential self from social restraints and conventions. The ideological and historical distinctions between these books obscure the underlying correspondences. Millett's understanding of Miller is best expressed not in the conventional perspectives of *Sexual Politics* but in the complex and contradictory field of consciousness that constitutes *Flying*.

A central concept in *Flying* is the pursuit of a version of liberation expressed as freedom from social and political obligation. This is seen as a necessary prerequisite of an independent existence, of the discovery of the real self: 'I will do it then, live my life, my own now maybe. I will be who I am. I must get that first, learn not through words but through feeling what that means. Then later I can go on, live for other people. If I have felt it enough. Lived it myself' (pp. 236–7). Ideology is, thus, concerned with the world of words; liberation (and art) is made from 'feeling what that means'. Political idealism is set against, and is a barrier to, the discovery of an essential instinctive self.

Miller and Millett are profoundly related by a sense that the drama of self-liberation is the essential material of creative expression. Millett's political sympathies are not vastly different from the kind of rage expressed in *Tropic of Capricorn*, where Miller exhibits a clear political sympathy for the dispossessed.[12] However, the real relationship in their work is based on a shared, paradoxical assumption that abandoning words for feelings is a necessary prerequisite of the revelation of self. That this process is recorded in, precisely, words is, of course, the heart of the paradox. It must also be said that this is an essentially Romantic paradox, but Miller and Millett express the resultant fertile ambiguity in a rich brew. Both *Flying* and *Tropic of Cancer* exploit the contradictions of the mobile consciousness as creative material.

The movement of the consciousness, expressed in Millett's metaphor of flying and Miller's image of the flow of a river, is a central subject. Millett's realisation that 'my existence is astonishing, dramatic' (p. 248) is a crucial identification of the source from which autobiographical fictions are made. It is clearly also Miller's source: 'The facts and events which form the chain of one's life are but starting points along the path of self-discovery. I have endeavoured to plot the inner pattern. . . .'[13] What is felt to be dramatic is not any sequence of events but the fluid, active, contradictory tensions embodied in the mobile consciousness. Millett's assertion in *Flying* that 'This book is myself' (p. 486) reveals a profound sympathy with the method of construction that characterises Miller's *Tropic of Cancer*.

There are, then, fundamental correspondences between *Flying* and *Tropic of Cancer*. The subject matter in both traces the discovery of an essential self in a state of liberation from social restraint and convention. They share a similar assumption that the consciousness itself is dramatic subject matter. That assumption is expressed, in, for example, Millett's rhetorical question 'Who will ever want to read this book, this collection of clutter in my mind?' The question is, of course, obliquely answered by the existence of the book itself, the doubt resolved by the act of completion and publication. The same resolution is implicit in *Tropic of Cancer*. The book encompasses the imperfections of 'clutter', is created out of the apparently non-selective, promiscuous movement of consciousness precisely because, in Miller's terms, it expresses 'the triumph of the individual over art' (p. 19). It thereby escapes, in Millett's terms, the tyranny of words.

Miller abandons the assumptions of literature as structured and selective experience and moves into the messy, cluttered areas of emotional complexity. The self is presented in debate with self, the consciousness in dramatic, often contradictory, movement. Miller's idea of self-collaboration as a mode of narrative is the source from which the work is made:

> Up to the present, my idea in collaborating with myself has been to get off the gold standard of literature. My idea briefly has been to present a resurrection of the emotions, to depict the conduct of a human being in the stratosphere of ideas, that is, in the grip of delirium.   (*Tropic of Cancer*, p. 244)

In Miller's work there is an attempt to embrace, represent and celebrate the fragmentary nature of experience. In a letter to Michael Fraenkel he sees this fragmentation as 'divine': 'And as for the "divine jumble", I adore it. I see nothing to be gained by straightening it out.'[14] Millett's 'clutter' and Miller's 'delirium' or 'divine jumble' are expressions of the fertile fields from which the narratives emerge. A central metaphor in these fields is that of exploration, which is an introspective rather than geographical process. In *Tropic of Capricorn*, for example, Miller argues that 'there is only one great adventure and that is inwards towards self, and for that, time nor space nor even deeds matter' (p. 11). The motif of flying that ends in Millett's vision of 'chaos and serenity together' (*Flying*, p. 162) is, like Miller's metaphor of movement and flow, an expression of the essential nature of journeying. Movement is finally not into geographical space but into the contradictory complexity of self.

The journey recorded in *Flying* is from a position of political and ideological obligation to the realisation that 'Finally all I had was who I am' (p. 487). There is throughout a tension between the public and the private self: 'Going home for two more speeches. The last ones. Always the last ones. Then free: never the public person again. Out of it, the vulgar insanity' (p. 5).

Tropic of Cancer begins precisely from that point that Millett aspires to, 'out of it', while *Tropic of Capricorn* describes the process of moving to that point. The narrator of *Tropic of Cancer* is a parody of that most American of archetypes, the self-made man. He is essentially an 'unmade man' who has cast off all sense of a public self; has become an embodiment of a consciousness without status or power, an appetite without obligation or responsibility: 'It is now the fall of my second year in Paris. I was sent here for a reason I have not yet been able to fathom. I have no money, no resources, no hopes. I am the happiest man alive' (p. 9). The narrator is passive, living in an environment that is, in a sense, a fictive idealisation of a world outside of life with its conventions, restraints and obligations. He is stripped of those accoutrements by which we define the social, public and political self. Thus the narrative voice can simultaneously assert 'we are dead' (p. 9) and 'Physically I am alive. Morally I am free. The world which I have departed is a menagerie' (p. 104). The 'deadness' of the narrator is a device by which Miller achieves dual objectives. It creates a consciousness freed from public existence, from 'life' in that sense. It also permits the establishment of an environment that moves between the real and the surreal. The simultaneous sense of the live and dead narrator offers a strategy in which Paris is both the real world of the American expatriate, and a landscape of dream and nightmare – a place of liberation and obsession that transcends the possibilities associated with the material world.

Miller's literary persona is, thus, a reversed Horatio Alger or a deconstructed Jay Gatsby. He embodies a profound alienation from the American ethos of material aspiration and upward social mobility. He manifests the political perspective that underlies Nathanael West's Lemuel Pitkin. West's figure in *A Cool Million* is literally 'dismantled', whereas Miller's figure is, in a more subtle sense, unmade and consequently, deeply, un-American.

The figure allows Miller to express a complete realisation of the process described in Millett's *Flying*. The world as a 'menagerie', and the attempt to escape the pressures of that world, is a common theme. This is apparent in *Tropic of Capricorn*, where Miller describes the imperatives of a working life that isolate the individual from the essential self. The world of work is a reductive pressure – a fundamentally destructive obligation. Millett, in contrast, suffers at the centre of a set of imperatives that emerge out of her political role within the feminist movement. In both *Flying* and *Tropic of Capricorn* additional imperatives afflict the narrators in the form of a family obligation. What unites both is the sense that they suffer pressures to adopt roles that are alien to an essential self. Thus the public stance is in direct conflict with private identity. The literary enterprise is both an expression of that conflict and an act of liberation in which the private self is asserted at the expense of the public persona. The public self, be it politically or domestically 'responsible', is progressively 'dismantled' in a process that finally reveals an essential self: naked, un-American and liberated.

At the heart of this process is the use that Miller and Millett make of sex and sexuality in their work. Sex is the mechanism through which the private or essential self is realised. It is a mode of action that expresses liberation from public roles, obligations and oppressive responsibilities. The naked self is literally and figuratively paramount in sexual action. The journey toward realisation of that self is a sexual one.

Inevitably, then, sexual action is closely related to philosophical exploration in the narratives. Miller sustains a complex and contradictory view of sexual action in *Tropic of Cancer*. The narrator moves between a view of sex as an act of sensual liberation, a metaphor for extreme social irresponsibility, and a version of sex as obsessional imprisonment. In *Sexus*,[15] for example, an orgy is the focus for a joyous rejection of all restraint: 'There was such a feeling of freedom and intimacy that any gesture, any act, became permissible' (p. 350). Simultaneously, however, the figure of June, in various guises, haunts Miller's fiction – as she haunted his life. The figure of June as Mara or Mona is expressed in a sequence of imperatives and disjunctions that form and transform experience into what comes close at times to surrealistic nightmare. Anais Nin, still the most perceptive critic of Miller's work, recognised the impact of June's emigmatic character: 'June's character seems to have no definable form, no boundaries, no core. This frightens Henry. He does not know all she is.'[16]

The transaction between Miller's life and art is well documented in, for example, Jay Martin's *Always Merry and Bright: The Life of Henry Miller*. In this context, however, the significance of June is that Miller translated the figure into part of the contradictory perspective on sexuality that is expressed in the fiction. As Nin saw, Miller transformed the real person into a fictional device:

> What was June? What was June's value? Henry loves her with passion, he wants to know June, the perpetually disguised woman. June, the powerful, fictionalized character. In his love for her he has endured so many torments that the lover took refuge in the writer.[17]

In that refuge, the relationship is used to express the obsessional nature of sex as reflected in a relationship that, in *Nexus*, Miller called 'an inferno of emotion'.[18] The contradiction is clear: sexual action is both an expression of liberation and freedom, and simultaneously the reverse, a prison of obsession. The contradiction is not between sex and love: both dimensions are integrated around the figure of Mara. In the orgy of *Sexus* involving Mara, Lola Jackson and Ulric, a sense of freedom from constraint and convention is sustained. The orgy liberates the participants from the concerns of their public selves as shown, for example, in the figure of Lola:

> Lola Jackson was a queer girl. She had only one defect – the knowledge that she was not pure white. That made her rather difficult to handle, at least in the preliminary stages. A little too intent upon impressing us with her culture and breeding. After a couple of drinks she unlimbered enough to show us how supple her body was. Her dress was too long for some of the stunts she was eager to demonstrate. We suggested that she take it off, which she did revealing a stunning figure which showed to advantage in a pair of sheer silk hose, a brassiere and pale-blue panties. Mara decided to follow suit. Presently we urged them to dispense with the brassieres. There was a huge divan on which the four of us huddled in a promiscuous embrace.   (p. 85)

The act of removing clothes corresponds to a casting-off of 'culture and breeding'. The public self is abandoned along with the underwear.

Sex is also used in Miller's work as a means of rejecting conventional moral standards. Sexual action is a rebellious gesture against a moral order that seeks to repress it. An orgy is a celebration of sensuality that, in Miller's version of a hostile America in *Sexus*, takes on the appearance, in the eyes of that society, of an 'outlaw' act. The narrator fantasies the interjection of that hostile moral order:

> It was too good to be true. I expected the door to be flung open any moment and an accusing voice scream: 'Get out of there, you brazen creatures.' But there was only the silence of the night, the blackness, the heavy sensual odours of earth and sex.   (p. 354)

The 'outlaw' nature of sexuality is, in a sense, a dramatic expression of what is essentially a Romantic philosophy expressed, for example, in an assertion that Miller makes to Michael Fraenkel in the 'Hamlet' correspondence: 'You've got to ally yourself with Nature, with instinct, with desire'.[19] That this state of alliance is an 'outlaw' act is part of the narrator's consciousness expressed in one version of sexual action. This version enacts what Miller called 'a real fight with the world'[20] and its rejected values.

This stance corresponds to Kate Millett's view that conventional morality and conventional sexual attitudes are oppressive. Both monogamy and heterosexuality are seen by Millett as the tools of a hostile moral order. They are those pressures from which the individual must seek liberation if the self is to be freed and realised.

The contradictions inherent in Miller's representation of sex are also expressed in Millett's work. Sex is seen as an ambiguous synthesis of liberation and obsession. Millett's *Sita* is, for example, a record of love transformed and distorted into shapes that approach nightmare:

> All love becomes vulnerability, the doorway to cruelty, the stairway to contempt. The very passion and adoration is now our undoing, the means of our evil. I in despising myself for loving, she in despising the one she had loved. Love turning back on itself, becoming its opposite.   (p. 22)

In one of its manifestations, love is for both Miller and Millett a dark anguish that broods over their work, threatening to become a nightmare inversion of itself. For Miller this anguish is largely focused in June, for Millett in *Sita*. An extreme revelation of this obsessional element in sex and love is expressed in Millett's *The Basement*, where she creates a fictional version of the real-life torture and murder of a young girl. The nightmarish abuse of the central figure is presented as depriving, in part, from perverse sexual obsession.

That version of sexuality coexists with a view that is entirely consistent with Miller's. In *Flying*, sexual action is, in one manifestation, a means of achieving the real self freed from oppressive obligations and imperatives. Sex leads to both liberation and insight into the nature of essential experience:

> And tonight blots out all the voices of my life, their squalid words hitting like stones: sin, perversity, infidelity, scandal.

Now I outcry them, certain, not only through joys of sense which in themselves become an ethic, but through a new perception that virtue, ultimately, is only another human being. Rejoicing in our bodies' woman's beauty, I can refute them, knowing that when I die I will have lived in these moments: when it comes to it, you have the world in your time, or you don't. Mine now is looking down on the gold of her head between my thighs while the white sky brings its first light through the ivy's green in the windows.   (p. 40)

In that sexual action, the violent intrusion of moral convention ('like stones') is transcended. The 'joys of sense' generate an ethic and lead, in a moment of lyrical epiphany, to a perception that reveals an essential self. The 'outlaw' nature of sex in Millett is enforced by the recorded attitudes of society towards lesbianism. Both Miller and Millett employ sex as a means of rejecting moral values and social conventions that are presented as hostile. They share a profound anti-Puritanism.

For both writers sex is also, as I have argued, a means of exploring paradox and contradiction. Neither seeks to resolve these, precisely because they share a view of art which is not dependent on structural cohesion or resolution. The field of literature is not the well-made, 'well-wrought urn', but the vast area of the active consciousness engaged in dramatic debate with self. Consequently, the narrative voice of *Flying* is consistent with that of *Tropic of Cancer* in so far as it is inclusive, promiscuous, ostensibly unedited. Millett's narrative voice is also radically different from the political/critical voice of *Sexual Politics*. Ideological rationality and political purpose give way to the greater energy of the creative voice in its paradoxical and contradictory exploration of the paradoxical and contradictory self. Anais Nin's description of her own and Miller's creative method applies equally to Millett's method of notebook narration in *Flying*:

Henry's recollections of the past, in contrast to Proust, are done while in movement. He may remember his first wife while making love to a whore, or he may remember his very first love while walking the streets, travelling to see a friend; and life does not stop while he remembers. Analysis in movement. No static vivisection. Henry's daily and continuous flow of life, his sexual activity, his talks with everyone, his café life, his conversations

with people in the streets, which I once considered an interrup-
tion to writing, I now believe to be a quality which distinguishes
him from other writers. . . .

It is what I do with the journal, carrying it everywhere, writing
on café tables while waiting for a friend, on the train, on the
bus, in waiting rooms at the station, while my hair is washed,
at the Sorbonne when the lectures get tedious, on journeys,
trips, almost while people are talking.[21]

Millett's description of her narrative method in *Flying* is an exact
reproduction of this technique: 'It's myself. It's a record as I go
along doing my thing' (p. 220). The book is comprised, as are Nin's
journals, of a sequence of notebooks which record 'analysis in
movement'. Miller's description of his method of narration, in a
letter to Anais Nin, clearly signals a similar technique:

If anybody had written a preface to it [*Tropic of Cancer*], they
might have explained that the book was written on the wing, as
it were, between my 25 addresses. It gives that sensation of
constant change of address, environment etc. Like a bad dream.
And for that it is good.[22]

This connection between movement and narrative voice leads
directly to a willingness to integrate contradiction into the fabric
of the text, and it makes juxtaposition the key to both styles. What
George Orwell called Miller's 'flowing, swelling prose'[23] is a product
of that procedure and that description is equally apt when applied
to Millett's autobiographical voice. It is precisely a promiscuous
voice that, in abandoning tight structure, creates a field of response
through which the self moves without restraint of logic or convention.

The subject matter is the 'naked' self and the self is, of course,
most naked, metaphorically and literally, in the sexual act. For
both writers, sex is given a dual function in the writing: it is used
to assert a rejection of the moral absolutes of a conventional society,
and it expresses an escape from the tyranny of time. A landscape
is created which offers an area of action beyond, and outside of,
material experience. Sex and love offer momentary transcendence
of a real and oppressive world. This moment is recorded in *Flying*:
'All time ceases, or is present together aloft in the sky like the two
incongruous lights sinking and rising but arrested now as we are

while we laugh or gaze or smoke, repeating our endless litany of love' (p. 583).

For Miller, in the opening of *Tropic of Cancer*, time similarly dissolves in the focus on Tania:

It is the twenty-somethingth of October. I no longer keep track of the date. Would you say – my dream of the 14th November last? There are intervals, but they are between dreams, and there is no consciousness of them left. The world around me is dissolving, leaving here and there spots of time. The world is a cancer eating itself away. . . . I am thinking that when the great silence descends upon all and everywhere music will at last triumph. When into the womb of time everything is withdrawn chaos will be restored and chaos is the score upon which reality is written. You Tania are my chaos. It is why I sing.   (p. 10)

The passage presents the focus of the desire as the 'chaos' that defeats, and exists outside of, time and the material world.

The narratives are able to move freely between sexual action and metaphysical introspection precisely because sexual action reveals a self that transcends the material world. Sex is seen to liberate the self from the gravity of social or political obligation, and the narrative voice thus floats freely into areas of philosophical speculation. Miller's concept of 'conversion' illustrates a direct transaction between the profane and the profound, between sex and introspection. The boundary between the two is eroded:

As to whether the sexual and the religious are conflicting and opposed, I would answer thus: every element or aspect of life, however necessitated, however questionable (to us), is susceptible to conversion, and indeed must be converted to other levels in accordance with our growth and understanding.[24]

There is, consequently, no contradition, in terms of the nature of the narrative, between a language of sexual description and a language of poetic or metaphysical intensity. Both narratives juxtapose these ostensibly contradictory idioms precisely because there is no felt contradiction between the sexual and the philosophical self. Miller's is the more dramatic juxtaposition:

I am fucking you Tania so that you'll stay fucked. And if you

are afraid of being fucked publicly I will fuck you privately.
I will tear off a few hairs from your cunt and paste them on
Boris' chin. I will bite into your clitoris and spit out two franc
pieces. . . .

Indigo sky swept clear of fleecy clouds, gaunt trees infinitely
extended, their black boughs gesticulating like a sleep walk.
Sombre, spectral trees, their trunks pale as cigar ash.

                                            (*Tropic of Cancer*, pp. 13–14)

Within the persona of the narrator, there is a movement from a
crude, violent sexual surrealism to a landscape invested, through
simile, with a sense of the moribund – a comatose world. The
explicit violence directed toward Tania is transformed by the
surrealist device, 'two franc pieces', into a dream sequence. Miller
exploits surrealist potential both to 'convert' violence into poetry
and to express the contradictions of the consciousness, and the
integration of those contradictions within the single self. Miller
presents the consciousness as a set of reconciled tensions valuable
in the dramatic intensity created. The stylistic mode of representing
this field of tension is the juxtaposition of the poetic and the
profane.

In less dramatic, more naturalistic form, Millett adopts the same
kind of movement. Arriving, for example, in New York, the
narrator in *Flying* moves from philosophical speculation to explicitly
sexual thought:

Improbable that the fantasy I was living before England could
support itself over time. A figment. Fictive. Most of all I inquire
of myself in the earsplitting pressure of landing, feeling very
New Yorker, most of all, am I gonna get laid?   (pp. 15–16)

As in Miller, the shift in idiom has a comic intention but it also
serves to enforce the sense of a literature built on the 'chaos'
of self. The organising principle is not selectivity or order but
inclusiveness. Millett's vision does not substantially differ from
Miller's view of what constitutes the subject matter of literary art:
'I said men, women and children. . . . They were all there, all
equally important. I might have added – books, mountains, rivers,
lakes, cities, forests, creatures of the air and creatures of the deep'.[25]
There is another correspondence between *Tropic of Cancer* and

Flying that relates directly to the theme of liberation. Both books express impulses that are common in American expatriate literature. They forge an image of Europe that exists as an alternative to American convention – a location in which the self can be freed from restraint. They also simultaneously sustain a sense of Europe as a landscape of cultural reference. America is the place of compulsion where the self is imprisoned. Europe is both freedom from that restraint and a place where the narrator engages with cultural complexity. Thus Millett's journey to Europe is a movement, literally and figuratively, from dark to light and an engagement with the past: 'All night the plane flies against time toward the east, America's blackness becoming light, the day moving back and now the dawn. The old world is ahead like the sunrise. Ruminate on tradition, Italy and England' (*Flying*, p. 271). From London, New York is a 'foreign madness' (p. 282). The same expatriate impulses pervade *Tropic of Cancer*. New York is 'cold, glittering, malign' (p. 74). America is described as 'a slaughter-house' (p. 39). In *Tropic of Capricorn*, Miller's Paris is, in contrast, an area of possibility where the narrator asserts, 'Everything happens here' (p. 27). It is also a place 'saturated with the past' (p. 317).

For both Miller and Millett, there is an unreality about Europe: the place of dream that is familiar in American perceptions of Europe. There is, for example, no substantial difference between Miller's version of Europe as 'golden peace' and Hawthorne's 'poetic or fairy precinct, where actualities would not be so terribly insisted upon as they are, and needs be, in America'.[26] The imperatives of social reality are suspended in the essentially conventional versions of the Old World created by Miller and Millett.

There is, however, a peripheral issue in this discussion. The basis of the relationship between Miller and Millett is that both writers assert the centrality of sex. For both, there is the notion of a real self which divests itself of gratuitous social, economic or political dimensions, and is revealed and celebrated in sexual action. In *Flying* Millett asserts, 'Nothing I could accomplish in life is such a cause for pride, a gratitude straining the heart to watch her come, great lovely head back in ecstasy' (p. 434). What Miller calls his 'night thoughts' lead toward the same conclusion, proposing the central importance of sex. Sex validates human activity: 'Ideas have to be wedded to action; if there is no sex, no vitality in them, there is no action' (*Tropic of Cancer*, p. 43). With these shared assumptions, Miller and Millett present sex as the pathway to enlightenment; the interactions between sex and introspection is not simply a literary strategy but the cornerstone of a shared cosmic view. Sex is, for both writers, what Miller called the 'omphalos' (*Tropic of Cancer*, p. 244), the central point of a system from which all else flows.

There is, then, a sense in which *Flying* contradicts the assertions of *Sexual Politics*. It goes beyond the ideological stance of that book and focuses on an inner self that seeks freedom from ideology and its imperatives. There is a further sense in which Millett's understanding of Miller is fuller and more perceptive in *Flying* than in *Sexual Politics*. In *Flying* she explores those areas of experience that transcend the ideologies of feminist criticism. She explores the same emotional landscape as Miller with the same tools. There is, as I have argued, a profound correspondence between the Millett of *Flying* and the Miller of *Tropic of Cancer*.

The Millett of *Sexual Politics*, the critical voice, approached Miller with a narrow perspective failing to recognise the comic persona of Miller's narrator. Anais Nin recognised that 'what Millett did was to take his humorous, comic stance seriously'.[27] Millett also failed, in Durrell's opinion, to identify Miller's real target: 'His obscenity is not brutality . . . what he's trying to do down is the dreadful sentimentality which disguises brutality.'[28]

The critical voice had other failures: the failure to recognise Miller's irony; the failure to recognise that *Tropic of Cancer* is, at least in part, a surrealistic foray into an underworld that has the texture of dream. Most significantly, perhaps, Millett failed to consider the distance between narrator and author, the degree to which Miller's work is not simply autobiography. This is signalled through the device of the 'deadness' of the narrator but it is also a distinction perceived by Miller himself, and not identified by Millett the critic:

> I have endeavoured to plot the inner pattern, follow the potential being who was constantly deflected from his course, who circled around himself, was becalmed for long stretches, sank to the bottom, or vainly essayed to reach the lonely, desolate summits. I have tried to capture the quintessential moments wherein whatever happened produced profound alterations. The man

telling the story is no longer the one who experienced the events recorded.[29]

However, the Millett of *Flying*, the creative voice, revealed a profound, if oblique, sympathy for Miller's position, and a deep insight into those characteristics of Miller's work that are beyond sexual politics.

On the ideological surface, Miller and Millett are strangers. Beyond ideology, in the innermost chambers of the contradictory heart, they both draw upon a rich vein of creativity which transcends issues of sexual politics and pornography. They share a capacity both to include experience and to transform it, to achieve, in Miller's words, an act of conversion out of which literary art is made: 'What seems nasty, painful, evil can become a source of beauty, joy and strength, if faced with an open mind.'[30]

NOTES

1. 'An Interview with Lawrence Durrell', interview with Frances Donnelly, 1 October 1985.
2. Walter Allen, *Tradition and Dream: The English and American Novel from the Twenties to our Time* (London: Phoenix House, 1964) p. 181.
3. Norman Mailer, *Genius and Lust: A Journey through the Major Writings of Henry Miller* (New York: Grove Press, 1976) p. 10.
4. Richard Hoggart, 'Art and Sex: the Rhetoric of Henry Miller', in *Speaking to Each Other*, vol. II: *About Literature* (London: Chatto and Windus, 1970) p. 102.
5. Kenneth Rexroth, 'The Reality of Henry Miller', in *Bird in the Bush: Obvious Essays* (New York: New Directions, 1959) p. 166.
6. Kate Millett, *Sexual Politics* (London: Virago, 1977) p. 313.
7. Ibid.
8. Ibid., p. 279.
9. Ibid., p. 295.
10. Kate Millett, *Flying* (St Albans, Herts: Paladin, 1974); *Sita* (London: Virago, 1977). Page references in the text.
11. Henry Miller, *Tropic of Cancer* (London: Panther, 1968). Page references in the text.
12. Henry Miller, *Tropic of Capricorn* (London: Panther, 1969). Page references in the text.
13. Henry Miller, *The World of Sex and Max and the White Phagocytes* (London: Calder and Boyars, 1970) p. 101.
14. Henry Miller, 'Letter to Michael Fraenkel, June 19, 1936', in *The Michael*

Fraenkel – Henry Miller Correspondence Called Hamlet (London: Carrefour, 1962) p. 171.

15. Henry Miller, *Sexus* (London: Panther, 1970). Page references in the text.
16. Anais Nin, *The Journals of Anais Nin*, vol. II (London: Quartet Books, 1973) p. 35.
17. Ibid., p. 48.
18. Henry Miller, *Nexus* (London: Granada, 1981) p. 68.
19. 'Letter to Michael Fraenkel, June 19, 1936' in *Fraenkel–Miller Correspondence*, p. 174.
20. Ibid., p. 175.
21. *Journals*, vol. I, p. 163.
22. Henry Miller, 'Letter to Anais Nin, May 3, 1934', in *Letters to Anais Nin*, ed. Gunther Stuhlmann (London: Peter Owen, 1965) p. 158.
23. George Orwell, 'Inside the Whale', in *Collected Essays* (London: Secker and Warburg, 1961) p. 123.
24. Miller, *The World of Sex*, p. 58.
25. Ibid., p. 66.
26. Nathaniel Hawthorne, *The Marble Faun* (London: Everyman, 1910) p. xv.
27. Anais Nin, 'The Unveiling of Woman', in *A Woman Speaks* (London: Star Books, 1982) p. 100.
28. 'An Interview with Lawrence Durrell', 1 October 1985.
29. Miller, *The World of Sex*, p. 101.
30. Ibid., p. 100.

9

Pope's Rape of Excess

LAURA CLARIDGE

As a feminist, I should have trouble enjoying *The Rape of the Lock*. After all, Pope cheerfully coerces woman into her proper social role as eighteenth-century men and, I would add, women defined it. Yet upon further scrutiny I find Pope's pinning of victim dependent upon a penning that undercuts its own potency, so that, rather than inscribing or circumscribing Belinda, the text instead suggests the inadequacy of Pope's pen to assume authority over her. For in her artifice, her mythic excess, Belinda exists beyond the close of the poem, unlike the Baron. Pope's mythology of female *jouissance* finally allows me to enjoy *The Rape of the Lock*, because the poem implies that woman's sexuality escaped definition and domestication; still, this male (and sometimes female) belief translates into the crippling position that, since woman's powers are so awesome, they must be contained. Ostensibly – and to most critics – a poem about the cheerful and necessary socialisation of a woman out of virginity, the covert psychological dynamic, sometimes at odds with other contexts the poet creates, is Pope's urge to 'virginalise' Belinda – to rid her of sexual power.

Creating the blank page of the virgin – the subject, for instance, of Susan Gubar's essay on Isaak Dinesen's story[1] – is Pope's goal in *The Rape of the Lock*, as virginal innocence keeps him safe from female creativity: Belinda as virgin versus Belinda as artful vessel. Art is veil, so that pulling back the veil, reducing art-inspired fantasies to the manageable, as Emily does in *The Mysteries of Udolpho*, is the meaning of the Baron's attempt 'to die' (v.78)[2] on Belinda. To rob Belinda of excess – to virginalise her or to make her plain – would assure Pope the power to name her, to exercise the male power of authorship. Pope fears Belinda's power as a creator: 'Let Spades be Trumps! she said, and Trumps they were' (III.46), she declares during a game of ompre, as Pope parodies God's act of creation in Genesis 1:3: 'Let there be light: and there

was light.' The act of artistic creation is in some ways analogous
to sexual intercourse, and the two processes were combined in a
metaphor common in seventeenth- and eighteenth-century satires
against women, wherein male poetic creations become 'weapons
aimed at squelching women's creative urges and denigrating those
creative urges by making them parallel to lascivious desires.'[3] Thus
Pope reappropriates generative power through his anxious claim
to superiority over the female. At the end of his poem, he tells
Belinda that he will make her immortal by writing her story; he
will create her, against the excess of sexuality that threatens to
overrun him. He will contain the female by inscribing her. In the
end, it is a modest goal: if successful, the task will merely leave
Belinda as impotent as Pope's man – not less, merely less than the
excess that is woman. For Belinda, unlike Samson, the loss of hair
only weakens her into equality with her violator; it does not destroy
her.

Ariel's exhortation to his charges that their task is 'To save the
powder from too rude a gale, / Nor let the imprisoned essences
exhale' (II.93–4) suggests that to keep the artificial intact is to avert
the rape, or, rather, that the rape would undo the artifice of the
seductress. To the extent that a woman is highly conscious of
herself as an object of desire, that is to say narcissistic, she presents
herself as a crafted product, an easy target for a poet's gaze. It is
this perspective that informs Pope's poem to Arabella Fermor and
Swift's boudoir poems as well. We ask, for instance, what purpose
the voyeuristic peep-hole at the dressing table serves in Swift's or
in Pope's poems; and we come to understand intrusion into the
boudoir as a case of the spectator engaged in watching an artist
construct, through her artful strategies, 'her sexual and psychic
independence as she creates a separate, private, and self-glorified
identity'.[4] Male participation at this point threatens to rob her of
that independence. Belinda, *as an object embodying Pope's fears of
woman*, enacts the position of woman as potential monster, a
'power less transcendent of nature than her male counterpart'[5] and
therefore more treacherous in her artifice, as it clearly is a disguise
for chaotic animal passion.

The high artifice of a carefully coiffed lock makes a perfect target
for a symbolic rape: the difficult is to be made simple. Indeed,
attending the rape are screams that are first compared to those
emitted when husbands or lapdogs are lost, but that issue equally
'when rich china vessels fallen from high, / in glittering dust and

painted fragments lie' (III.159–60) – when art, that is, or the vessels, loses its monopoly on complex meaning. To virginalise Belinda is the covert agenda of this poem in the sense that to expropriate from art its multivalence allows the interpreter to reduce it to what is clear, a goal perhaps congruent with an eighteenth-century emphasis upon correctness. Belinda is artful; her 'signified', the measurable, is veiled so heavily that her origin seems unclear. The conjunction of female and art is terrible: imitating life, they both exceed it as well. Both deliver the child, the final product – though monstrously, extravagantly, the female grows the child within.

Art-ifice and art-full-ness in woman must be dismantled, whether in Swift's boudoir poems or in Pope's *Rape*. And *The Rape of the Lock* is an artful poem: Belinda develops her artifice from the 'glitt'ring Spoil' of the world, which is strange and exotic:

This casket *India's* glowing Gems unlocks,
And all *Arabia* breathes from yonder Box.
The Tortoise here and Elephant unite,
Transformed to *Combs*, the speckled and the white.
(I.130–6)

Woman's art threatens male artistry as this latter mode is itself a substitute for the creative act of bearing a child: the artist bears the word or image with the pen or brush instead. When woman appropriates this mode, the man is truly castrated and bereft, since now the mother has the phallus after all. Belinda as 'painted vessel' (II.47), the orifice hidden from the eye, invites the appropriating gaze. Her artifice keeps her non-literal, hence unmeasurable, thus dangerous. The very slipperiness of art can threaten the viewer, so that a temptation exists toward closure in the act of interpretation. Paradoxically, this elusiveness is often what constitutes the compelling quality of what we name great art, as in the enigma of the Mona Lisa's smile, or the playfulness of Seurat's dots, or the dissolve of Monet's borders. Hence an anxiety for Pope – and here also the tension that keeps the poem from ending as an anti-female text; Belinda as 'painted vessel' threatens to surpass the gazer's powers of definition – to surpass Pope's power of penning Belinda in – because of the artifice that the poet necessarily denounces even as he is attracted to it.

This slipperiness of art, then, turns out to be emblematic of woman's covert power. Art is dangerous in part because it can trick as it creates illusion, as with the paradoxical 'purer Blush' (1.143) that Belinda effects through her cosmetics. As canto II begins, Belinda's eyes are 'unfix'd' as she sails up the Thames in a scene explicitly contrasting her appearance with the competing natural glory of nature. Belinda's art is so dangerous that her artfully constructed face can cause us to 'forget' 'Female Errors' (II.17, 18); in fact, this face conduces to the 'Destruction of Mankind' (II.19). She is a trap: in yet another slippage of gender, Belinda's strength in her hair becomes Samson-like, capable of bringing down the temple:

> Fair Tresses Man's Imperial Race in snare,
> And Beauty draws us with a single Hair.
> (II.27-8)

After all, artifice allows for obstruction of the truth: Belinda smiles and all the world is gay (II.52), regardless of what wretches hang so that judges can get to dinner (III.21-3). That this treachery of artifice is associated particularly with the powers of female vessels is clear in the opening of canto III, which highlights the ease with which a woman-as-ruler can slip between two disparate, almost mutually cancelling, roles:

> Here Thou, Great *Anna*! whom three Realms obey,
> Dost sometimes Counsel take – and sometimes Tea.
> (III.7-8)

Art is a form of metonymy, as it always is a part pointing to a whole, an object allowing for larger interpretation. And metonymy, as it implies absence, is desire, as Lacan says, so that art equals desire, and Belinda equals art, and this poem is of Pope's desire of her desire.[6]

Belinda's artfulness makes her stability as truth-teller suspect. She signs to an audience a cue, which they interpret, basing their conclusion on the hope that Belinda as signifier is true. Even the sylphs, Belinda's army of supporters, appear as threateningly infinite, finally unrepresentative in nature:

> Transparent forms too fine for mortal sight,
> Their fluid bodies half dissolved in light . . .

While every beam new transient colours flings,
Colours that change whene'er they wave their wings.
(II.61–2, 67–8)

In this world of conflated gender, the sylphs 'Assume what Sexes
and what Shapes they please' (I.70); spirits of dead coquettes, the
sylphs remind us of the ways in which women function as
transparent signifiers who transport meaning for others: they wait
upon meaning, whether to be filled with child or penis or pen.
That the sylphs are most often male points to Pope's interesting
experiments with gender-swapping (as with the pregnant man in
the Cave of Spleen), in which the male becomes imbued with
something typically female, whether child or maternal phallus.

Psychologically, if creation with the pen substitutes for creation
with the womb – the real, rather than imaginary, act of generation –
to the extent that a woman appropriates that male substitution,
she truly looms as the phallic mother, the one who has it all, womb
and phallus and power. We might call to mind Charles Kirkpatrick
Sharp's watercolour of the Cave of Spleen: what is it that Belinda
possesses to cause others to want it so much that their desire
looks monstrous?[7] It is certainly not her tresses – not even her
maidenhead – but it is the peculiar power that accrues to standing
outside the social order. Artists who desire aesthetic authenticity
in a pure 'language' envy the silence and subversion implicit in
woman's excess, their otherness, their finally defensive *jouissance*.
And monstrous men want to rape that power, while nice men
want to share in it – to have babies, as in the Cave of Spleen –
though, even imaginatively, women often jealously guard this
generative power for themselves. Felicity Nussbaum describes
Robert Gould's *Love Given O'er* as an explanation for women's
insatiable sexuality, so that the 'inevitable rhyme for "womb" is
"tomb"'.[8] This association points to a male fear of generativity, or
the power of it, run wild, especially as it incapacitates the man. In
canto v of *The Rape of the Lock* an illustrative juxtaposition of three
lines occurs:

[The Baron] sought no more than on his Foe to die.
But this bold Lord, with manly strength indu'd
She with one Finger and a Thumb subdu'd.
(v.77–9)

The pun on sexual consummation ('to die'), contiguous with
Belinda's strength – all-powerful in its putative weakness – prepares
us for the lines soon following, where the finiteness of male desire
(the visible detumescence of potency) contrasts with the infinite
female desire, as the Baron asks that his desire become as a
woman's:

> Boast not my Fall (he cry'd) insulting Foe!
> Thou by some other shalt be laid as low.
> Nor think, to die dejects my lofty Mind;
> All that I dread, is leaving you behind!
> Rather than so, ah let me still survive,
> And burn in *Cupid's* Flames, – but burn alive!
> (v.97–102)

Accordingly, Pope's project in *The Rape of the Lock* is to take back
the pen(is) from the artful Belinda, to show her who the real artist
of definition is. One reason why a feminist can enjoy this poem is
that the man as voyeuristic writer does not have the penis either,
only the pen. He is in lack – that is, he desires – as does Belinda.
Indeed, as theorists of desire as disparate as Jacques Lacan and
René Girard would insist, Pope's desire is triangular, for, even as
he allows the Baron to revel in obtaining the mother's phallus ('the
glorious Prize is mine! . . . So long my Honour, Name, and Praise
shall live' III, 162, 170), he takes it back, as he allows the lock to
ascend into a poet's penned heaven. Desire, as it constantly
attempts to express itself and to achieve consummation and yet
revel in infinite deferral, retains the property of a signifier, the
most slippery one of them all.

I am suggesting, then, that we can read Pope's poem (and derive
meaning previously obscured) as a defence against his – that is,
eighteenth-century – fear of female strength, which becomes
translated into a prejudice against what we might term aesthetic
excess, that which escapes control. Metonymic women is violated
because she exceeds what she makes available to others: she is
open to interpretation. The abnormal energy – almost a voyeuristic
panting – that infuses Thalestris's speech to Belinda in the middle
of canto IV gives away Pope's hand. For her is Pope's desire
speaking itself – the real rape:

Methinks already I your Tears survey,
Already hear the horrid things they say,
Already see you a degraded Toast,
And all your Honour in a Whisper lost!
How shall I, then, your helpless Fame defend?
(iv.107–11)

The poet has exposed Belinda and made her vulnerable as she loses part of her artfully constructed self, in order to nullify her. Now he will use the artifice of her story to build himself up – to make potent his pen with her stolen phallic power, the rape whose economy drives the narrative. If the male's sexual potency is palpable, measurably undependable – finally, that is, phallic – women's hidden, recessed (and hence unmeasurable) potency threatens to exceed the phallus, to mimic the *jouissance* of St Teresa's ecstasy, that which, as Lacan tells us, dares to become mystical and therefore to mystify our concept of woman. Even when 'Woman's transient Breath is fled' (1.51), she still possesses the phallus – she still 'o'erlooks the Cards' (1.54), the game which, in this poem, enacts sexual contest and triumph most fully, especially as it is the game in which Belinda indeed holds the phallus, the Ace of Spades.

Pope's style itself conveys his concern with controlling excess. The heroic couplet, unfeminine in its severe closure, and formally imitative of the tumescent wax and wane of male phallic arousal, works to contain the hyperbole of the verses. When we read 'What dire offence from amorous causes springs, / What mighty contests rise from trivial things' (1.1–2) we are alerted to the parodic intent of the text; yet the serious truths cannot fail to suggest themselves too: Helen of Troy, Cleopatra, Salome, Judith, Delilah, Catherine the Great – all examples of the phallic (male and female) contest of power rising precisely from seemingly trivial things, the wish to complete desire, to consummate the minor irritation of sexual arousal. That sex and power can never be divorced is evident from the beginning of Pope's poem, and in the hyperbole in which he couches this truth we sense the desire that outstays his pen:

Slight is the subject, but not so the praise,
If *she inspire*, and he approve my lays.
(1.5–6, emphasis added)

Here Pope does three things: he asserts the triviality of the subject (Belinda herself?); he assigns Belinda's powers to the imaginary (she inspires); and he implies that the man's potency clearly lies within the measurable realism of the law (his it is to approve or disapprove). Six lines later, the couplet points again to the female 'extra' which threatens to overcome the merely quantifiable:

In tasks so bold can little men engage,
And in soft bosoms dwell such mighty rage?
(I.11–12)

These lines read oddly; again, the consistent formal demand is for parody, yet only the first phrase is truly parodic: after all, the task of cutting the hair is obviously trivial, not bold, so that, indeed, only 'little men' would see it as large. And in the soft bosom mighty rage did dwell, or there would not be occasion for this poem, as Pope himself clearly recognises. A retrospective reading of the first phrase, given that what appears in the following phrases initially to continue the parodic intent actually merely tells the story, invites us to understand the first phrase too – 'task so bold' – as merely forwarding the narrative, so that for 'little men' the task of appropriating female power is in truth not parody but a formidable, 'bold' one.

Pope's excessively controlled wordplay in fact suggests an excess of energy that he pins down either in syntax or in images of libido run wild:

Oft, when the world imagines women stray,
The Sylphs through mystic mazes guide their way,
Through all the giddy circle they pursue,
And old impertinence expel by new.
What tender maid but must a victim fall
To one man's treat, but for another's ball?
When Florio speaks what virgin could withstand,
If gentle Damon did not squeeze her hand?
(I.91–8)

Even the wordplay of the famous zeugma suggests a world out of control just as it is extremely overcontrolled – that is, the exaggerated linguistic tightness points to a defence against its opposite:

Where wigs with wigs, with sword-knots, sword-knots strive,
Beaux banish beaux, and coaches coaches drive.

(I.101–2)

This paradoxical implication of chaos adumbrates the confusion in the Cave of Spleen, where a world raped of order is imaged in inversions of the 'natural' way of things.

'Unnaturalness' always clings to Belinda, however, even without the Cave of Spleen. The *jouissance* that makes her independent of man's sexual offerings surfaces in the erotic use of Shock, the lapdog, particularly as Shock stands in for the male. Ariel warns Belinda of the great danger awaiting her at the hands of man, but immediately, with some narrative disjunction, his warning is meliorated by Shock's action: he leaps up and wakes his mistress with his tongue. Whatever Shock's libidinous urges, however, there is never any doubt that Belinda uses him as an object – as Lacan's *petit objet à* – for her own pleasure, but to be brushed off her lap when she loses desire for him. As Robert Halsband discusses, lapdogs were assumed in this period to have 'erotic connotations'. Furthermore, Pope's Rosicrucian sources for the sylphs included the 'notion that sylphs sometimes took on the shapes of dogs',[9] with the implication present in the Rosicrucian sources of the period that some women had unnaturally close relationships with their dogs. The dog as equivalent of male sexuality in this poem (for instance, immediately following the rape there is a reference to a time 'When husbands, or when lapdogs breathe their last' – III.158) suggests the wild, errant, uncontrolled nature of Belinda's subversive desire, as well as reducing man's sexuality to that of an easily manageable pet. Furthermore, the very perversity of the lapdog as object of desire emphasises the artifice, the unnaturalness, the threat of art in the world which Pope creates.

The contest of sexual power in this poem speaks most persuasively through the multiple echoes of the word 'steel'. Importantly situated at the climax and end of canto III, as emblem for the rape itself, it is the 'unresisted' metal of the scissors that becomes the 'conquering force' over Belinda's lock. But the image of forcing open a lock with scissors suggests the voyeuristic, the gaze, the ocular act of taking a picture in and then feeling it a part of oneself – of looking through the peephole of the lock that one would force open. And why is the steel 'unresisted'? Literally, the hair offers no resistance; it is, ostensibly, an easy target, which thus automatically derogates the manliness implicit in force. But, more problematic, the steel may be 'unresisted' because the hair wants to be cut too. And while Pope uses this implication to seduce Belinda–Arabella into assuming her proper social role as wife and commodity, there also slips in the truth again of woman having it however she wants – with the Baron, with the scissors, with the dog. 'Steel' – a word laden with the sound of theft: what is being stolen? Far more than virginity: this is the attempted theft of femaleness, of power that far exceeds the literal state of the hymen. It is a Promethean theft. Paradoxically, we could even suggest that, rather than stealing Belinda's virginity, the Baron seeks her fertility – to castrate her into *being* a virgin. And later, with her own steel, her bodkin, Belinda threatens the Baron: meant, of course, to trivialise Belinda, yet in the lineage that Pope offers for the bodkin – tracing it through generations of grandparents and babies – it suggests the overflow of procreative power that accretes to the female, that which outlives any single appropriating act of force (v.87–96).

Indeed, male anxiety to keep up with the desire of woman – or to keep it up – surfaces throughout the poem. Pope's Baron (or *barren* or *bearone*) builds an altar to Love, an altar of past conquests: three garters, half a pair of gloves, and billets-doux with which he lights the fires. Love letters, whether written to Belinda or to the Baron, are signifiers of desire, and in fact the erotic nature of the text, the rhythm of writing, enacts Pope's concept of the desires of woman that permeates this poem. Certainly the Baron's worship is couched in obviously sexual terms of male physical arousal: he 'breathes three amorous sighs to raise the fire' before the 'prostrate altar' and 'begs' to 'obtain' and 'possess the prize' (II.42–4). The Baron's nameless name encourages the pun on 'barren', on childless – lacking, that is, the female phallus, the child, so that the image in the Cave of Spleen of the pregnant man is pregnant with meaning.[10]

Certainly, to the extent that woman is perceived as a (potentially pregnant) vessel, she is a signifier who, on the one hand, promises to point to origin, and, on the other, suggests the danger of trying to fix meaning. Thus the game of ombre in canto III, where cards shift in meaning, holding significance only in relation to other cards, tells the story of signifiers always in excess of the signified. Man is the literal baby the woman bears, but the woman is the bearer of meaning, so that her shifting of position, her fluctuating desire, grants paternity and authenticity, in spite of the male attempt to share in that power by calling the gestation of her desire by his name. Thus that which is only signifier, only vessel or conduit, becomes the unveiled phallus of origin and meaning as well. For by now we have come to see that a competition exists in this poem between the (if none the less illusory) real and the interpretative, or unstable: between signified and signifier. Appearance wins out over reality enough to acquaint us with Pope's own anxiety over the power of art: at court, languid gentlemen and ladies interpret 'Motions, Looks, and Eyes' so that 'at ev'ry Word a Reputation dies' (III.15, 16). Meanwhile, 'Judges soon the Sentence sign, / And Wretches hang that Jury-men may dine' (III.21–2). Immediately following these two censures of interpretative powers in defining the real, Belinda appears, 'And swells her Breast with Conquests yet to come' (III.28) – Belinda as castrater, as all too artful herself. A strong position in this poem, not that it is necessarily Pope's intention, is that it is not the real, the signified, that counts, but appearances, signifiers, *artifice* – or interpretation – that do:

> Oh hadst thou, Cruel! been context to seize
> Hairs less in sight, or any Hairs but these!
> (IV.175–6)

And, as Ellen Pollak points out, as a 'Vessel' (II.47) laden with 'glitt'ring Spoil' (I.132), Belinda functions as 'at once the bearer of ornament and an ornament herself'.[11]

Yet, in spite of the myth of female power that covertly informs *The Rape of the Lock*, cantos IV and V threaten to spoil my pleasure with the whole. Belinda's prize, her art, is to be 'Exposed through crystal to the gazing eyes' (IV.13–14), as, of course, the real Belinda's art will be on display to any eyes perusing Pope's text. Pope will translate Arabella's story into a text that increases his powers, just as the Baron will wear Belinda's hair: a man gaining potency through raping a women of her strength, a strength he ostensibly mocks. Pope's art will surpass the woman's generational power, as he keeps her alive with his craftsmanship:

> For after all the Murders of your Eye,
> When, after Millions slain, your self shall die;

When those fair Suns shall set, as set they must,
And all those Tresses shall be laid in Dust;
This Lock, the Muse shall consecrate to Fame,
And mid'st the Stars inscribe *Belinda's* Name!
(v.145–50)[12]

It is in cantos IV and V that we feel the true nature of rape as appropriation, as a desperate attempt to steal the femaleness that threatens those it excludes, Clarissa or the Baron.

Indeed, the critical discomfort with Clarissa – is she a mouthpiece of the author's, conveying the moral message, or a prude, or a jealous would-be object of the Baron's affection? – helps us to understand these cantos. Clarissa is a man, in gender, of course, not in sex: her weapon, the scissors, are 'two-edged' (III.128) because she rejects *jouissance*, overflow, and instead helps the Baron rape Belinda's lock, after which she dares to condemn Belinda's resentment. Clarissa reads as male in this text because she is too simple, in the world and context which Pope creates, to be female. She lacks the sexual complexity thought to be female, which is the covert object of admiration and of violence in this poem. One could say that she *is* a virgin – paradoxically, that she has been denuded – and that she is not less than man, but equal to him, to the Baron, in this poem.

Maynard Mack rightly emphasises the importance to *The Rape of the Lock* of Sarpedon's speech in Pope's translation of Homer, for it is parodied in Clarissa's exhortation to Belinda. Yet the implications of the parody are more subtle, psychologically, than Mack or even Pope might have recognised. Through Sarpedon, Homer defines the 'curve of action begun in glory and closed by death (repeated again and again in the poem) that defines the heroic code';[13] but sexuality is a series of little deaths that *never* close the conflict and that repeat themselves again and again as desire seeks consummation only to be rekindled. Thus marriage, which is what Clarissa really urges in the parody of Sarpedon's speech, allows for the kind of control and heroic closure to chaotic desire that Belinda and her lapdog represent: marriage defines a hero's endeavours by conferring meaning upon the chaos of sexual energy. It is the earnestness with which Pope proffers this 'solution' that meliorates the otherwise off-putting part that Clarissa plays in the poem. As Mack illustrates, Pope seemed to have entertained a genuine concern for the plight of women in his society: he intervened on behalf of married women who were mistreated by their husbands, and, at least in one work, his early 'To a Young Lady, with the Works of Voiture' – he emphasises the tyrannical 'forms' by which society binds women, both before and after marriage.[14] If, as Mack surmises, Pope's infatuation with the coquettish Teresa Blount infuses *The Rape of the Lock*, we can conclude that his ambivalence in the poem over Belinda's eroticism comes in part because he truly worried over Teresa's refusal to emphasise anything but the material, even as her sensuality snared him in its voluptuousness.

The last two cantos, then, lack the convincing poetic seductiveness to engage a feminist reader because Pope rapes Belinda of her power to create the desire of the poem – her desire becomes *his* poem, to his glory. By the end of canto v, it is clear that Belinda's fame will be sounded only because of Pope: he will impose the symbolic, organising power of language upon her errant, 'unfixed' eye (II.10), and fix her with his pen. It is interesting here to juxtapose the *Rape*'s conclusion with the 'Epistle to Mr Jervas', where Pope explicitly commends the power of art to sustain the beauty which otherwise dies:

> Yet still her charms in breathing paint engage;
> Her modest cheek shall warm a future age.
> Beauty, frail flow'r that ev'ry season fears,
> Blooms in thy colours for a thousand years.
>
> (II.55–8)

As he continues, he invokes the Blount sisters and, more surprisingly, his heroine in *The Rape of the Lock*: 'Each pleasing Blount shall endless smiles bestow, / And soft *Belinda's* blush for ever glow' (II.61–2). Clearly, male art can circumscribe the female. Still, what finally saves *The Rape of the Lock* for my feminist sensibilities is that Pope's privileging of his authorial powers still cannot overcome the vestiges of a sense of female sexual imaginary potency which Pope creates. Pope does not have the last word, for desire's nature is to ignite itself continuously, and thus Belinda exists, as Keats defines art in his 'Ode on a Grecian Urn', to be violated again and again; to function, that is, as a sign of the extra that signifies woman, unpinnable, and penned in full by no one. Belinda's *jouissance* in the first three cantos exceeds Pope's power of the pen to inscribe her wholly within the last two.

In conclusion, we are left with one important distinction to maintain, that between the world of the poem and the world of our own lives today. In speaking of an excess of energy, of signification, of female organisation of life that exceeds the rational, we immediately use outdated terms that in the past encouraged a dangerous mystification of woman that kept her, in far too many ways, weak. But, while I am unwilling to grant to woman a primal inherent *jouissance* that sex alone confers, I am also unwilling to deny the possibility that culture has done, in a historically compensatory way, what biology had no rationale for doing. What seems certain to me, at any rate, is that a psychological drama which defends Pope, and others of his time, against the uncanny power that seemed to reside in a politically powerless creature – eighteenth-century woman – constitutes at least one level of his famous narrative. Just as dreams play out several scripts all at the same time, *The Rape of the Lock* tells more stories than the one for which it is famous.

NOTES

1. Susan Gubar, ' "The Blank Page" and the Issues of Female Creativity', *The New Feminist Criticism* (New York: Pantheon, 1985).
2. All citations of Pope's poetry come from *The Twickenham Edition of the Poems of Alexander Pope*, ed. J. Butt *et al.*, 11 vols (London: Methuen, 1938–68). Quotations from *The Rape of the Lock* are identified by canto and line(s).
3. F. Nussbaum, *The Brink of All We Hate: English Satires on Women 1660–1750* (Lexington: University of Kentucky Press, 1984) p. 37.
4. Ibid., p. 105.
5. B. Kowaleski-Wallace, 'Milton's Daughters: the Education of Eighteenth-Century Women Writers', *Feminist Studies*, 12, no. 2 (Summer 1986) 287.
6. My reference to Lacanian concepts of desire and to Lacan's schema of the imaginary, symbolic and real are based on J. Lacan, *Ecrits*, tr. Alan Sheridan (New York: Norton, 1977), and J. Lacan, *The Four Fundamental Concepts of Psycho-Analysis*, tr. Alan Sheridan (New York: Norton, 1981).
7. For a reproduction of this painting by Fuseli's disciple see R. Halsband, *'The Rape of the Lock' and its Illustrations 1714–1896* (Oxford: Clarendon Press, 1980) p. 66.
8. Mussbaum, *The Brink of All We Hate*, p. 29.
9. Halsband, *'The Rape of the Lock' and its Illustrations*, p. 11.
10. Male impregnation is a fantasy in other satires: Richard Ames's 'The

Folly of Love', for instance, creates a male Utopia where men procreate unaided by women (Nussbaum, *The Brink of All We Hate*, p. 40). That this poem, as Nussbaum notes, bears certain similarities to Swift's 'A Beautiful Young Nymph Going to Bed' is significant in the intersection of desire, gender and generativity that Restoration and eighteenth-century satire promote.

11. Ellen Pollak, *The Poetics of Sexual Myth* (Chicago: University of Chicago Press, 1985) p. 95.
12. Similarly, if in a less conscriptive manner, the conflation of desire and the pen, or Muse, which can keep even a dead woman alive, is present in Pope's 'Elegy to the Memory of an Unfortunate Lady'.
13. Maynard Mack, *Alexander Pope: A Life* (New York: Norton, 1985) p. 131.
14. Ibid., pp. 239–41.

10

Wayward Girls but Wicked Women?

Female Sexuality in Angela Carter's *The Bloody Chamber*

AVIS LEWALLEN

Wayward Girls and Wicked Women is the ironic title for a volume of short stories written by women, edited by Angela Carter, and published by Virago in 1986. The title, cover picture (sulky, seductive, tousled blond with pouting red lips, bare shoulders and plunging neckline) and editor's name (a writer with a reputation for polemic) signify sexuality as the subject under scrutiny. The back cover blurb does nothing to dispel this impression. In her Introduction to the volume Angela Carter explains the irony:

> To be a wayward girl usually has something to do with pre-marital sex; to be a wicked woman has something to do with adultery. This means it is far easier for a woman to lead a blameless life than it is for a man; all she has to do is to avoid sexual intercourse like the plague. What hypocrisy!

The majority of the stories, therefore, have little to do with sexuality *per se* and are about women facing their economic, social and sexual inequality with bravado, perseverance or at times perversity. The package promises something different from what it actually contains, and, though some of the stories are enjoyable, it is the cover, in what it reveals about the marketing practices of a feminist publishing house in relation to the supposed expectations of its readership, that is especially interesting. Sexy covers and titles sell books, even to women. Similarly, Angela Carter's own writing has a surface gloss and shimmer. Recently dubbed 'the high priestess of post-graduate porn,'[1] she has provocative ideas and a seductive style, but closer analysis reveals a dubious kind of sexuality for women.

The Bloody Chamber examines sexuality for women as victims within a misogynistic society, and in some ways this collection of tales is a fictional rendering of the ideas Carter expounds in her theoretical analysis of the works of the Marquis de Sade, *The Sadeian Woman*.[2] In this she posits the notion of a 'moral pornographer':

> His business would be the total demystification of the flesh and the subsequent revelation, through the infinite modulations of the sexual act, of the real relations of man and his kind. Such a pornographer would not be the enemy of women, perhaps because he might begin to penetrate to the heart of the contempt for women that distorts our culture even as he entered the realms of true obscenity as he describes it. . . . And that is because sexual relations between men and women always render explicit the nature of social relations in the society in which they take place and, if described explicity, will form a critique of those relations, even if that is not and never has been the intention of the pornographer.[3]

Thus Sade, Carter argues, provides such a critique, exposing the political reality behind sexual mythology, while 'he declares himself unequivocally for the right of women to fuck'.[4] Claiming and practising this right 'aggressively, tyrannously and cruelly'[5] is, therefore, a historical process that has to be gone through before any kind of equalisation can be reached between the sexes. Perhaps the problem with this argument is that Carter herself does not have a sufficient historical perspective to recognise the sixties and the seventies as a period when women did claim their right to fuck. Such 'liberalisation' has partly resulted in a circumspect cynicism towards the notion of any sexual equality within the pervasive patriarchal system.

Ironically, Carter and one of her critics, Andrea Dworkin, both give supreme importance and power to this one aspect of sexual representation. I would not argue that pornographic representation is not important, but would say that it must be placed within the context of all forms of sexual representation. Some of these forms such as advertisements which utilise pornographic images, may, by the very fact of their seeming 'naturaliness', be more pernicious. Pornography in Carter's and Dworkin's sense is the raw and extreme form of sexual representation and is underlined by more pervasive ideologies concerning female sexuality. It is hard to see that it can do more than perpetrate myths in a very obvious way, instead of, as Carter suggests, critically exposing the heart of misogyny.

Sade's dualism is simple: sadist or masochist, fuck or be fucked, victim or aggressor – never one and the same but always either/or. This is Sade's failure, claims Carter, because sex as described by him is always sequential and never mutually reciprocal. It is this dualism that pervades our thinking about sexuality and fits neatly into the schema of binary oppositions: subject/object, active/passive, and so forth. In *The Bloody Chamber* Carter is attempting to promote an active sexuality for women within a Sadean framework, and, therefore, within the logic of the world she creates, sexual choice for the heroines is circumscribed by Sadean boundaries. One wonders why, given her recognition of what she sees as Sade's failure, there is no attempt to address the question of these ideologically defined parameters.

The Bloody Chamber is mostly a collection of fairy tales rewritten to incorporate props of the Gothic and elements of a style designated 'magic realism', in which a realistic consciousness operates within a surrealistic context. The characters are at once both abstractions and 'real'. The heroine in 'The Tiger's Bride', for example, bemused by surreal events, comments, 'what democracy of magic held this palace and fir forest in common? Or, should I be prepared to accept it as proof of the axiom my father had drummed into me: that, if you have enough money, anything is possible?' (p. 62). Symbolism is prevalent: white roses for sexual purity; lilies for sex and death; lions, tigers and wolves for male sexual aggression. Throughout the collection, specific attention is often drawn to the meaning of fairy tales themselves, and this has implications for the reading of Carter's stories.

In a perceptive but highly critical essay Patricia Duncker argues that the form of the fairy tale, along with all its ideological ramifications, proves intractable to attempted revision:

Carter is rewriting the tales within the strait-jacket of their original structures. The characters she re-creates must, to some extent, continue to exist as abstractions. Identity continues to be defined by role, so that shifting the perspective from the impersonal voice to the inner confessional narrative, as she does in several of the tales, merely explains, amplifies and reproduces rather than alters the original, deeply, rigidly sexist psychology of the erotic.[6]

While I agree with Duncker's overall analysis, I think she significantly overlooks the use of irony, particularly the effect produced by the 'inner confessional narrative', which both acknowledges patriarchal structure and provides a form of critique against it. The ultimate position taken up may be politically untenable, but at the same time the ironic voice does not wholeheartedly endorse the patriarchal view. I think the use of irony can clearly be illustrated by the two contrasting versions Carter offers of 'Beauty and the Beast'.

Both 'The Courtship of Mr Lyon' and 'The Tiger's Bride' draw attention to the economic dependence of the daughter on the father/husband. 'The Courtship of Mr Lyon' conforms in most respects to the traditional 'Beauty and the Beast' narrative. Beauty's father is bankrupt, but a chance meeting with the mysterious Mr Lyon, who is indeed a lion, provides a means of restoring his fortunes. The unspoken price for this benevolence is Beauty herself, but she is a price that can be exacted only through love, not through direct contract or guilt. Material exchange underlies the narrative, but it is somewhat obscured by Beauty's feelings of pity for Mr Lyon, tinged with unease about the sexuality in the beast which might also be sexuality within herself:

> How strange he was. She found his bewildering difference from her almost intolerable; its presence choked her . . . and when she saw the great paws lying on the arm of his chair, she thought: they are the death of any tender herbivore. And such a one she felt herself to be, Miss Lamb, spotless, sacrificial. (p. 45)

Mr Lyon's 'strangeness' – his sexual difference – repels, frightens but also attracts: 'It was in her heart to drop a kiss upon his shaggy mane but, though she stretched out her hand towards him she could not bring herself to touch him of her own free will, he was so different from herself' (p. 48). With her father's fortunes restored, Beauty joins him in the city, which is in danger of corrupting her innocence, making her vain and causing her to forget her promise to return to Mr Lyon. She experiences contradictory feelings:

she experienced a sudden sense of perfect freedom, as if she had just escaped from an unknown danger, had been grazed by the possibility of some change but, finally, left intact. Yet, with this exhilaration, a desolating emptiness.   (p. 48)

Through a kind of oxymoronic yoking of feelings Carter conveys the hesitancy of burgeoning sexuality. We are reminded through style and structure of Mills and Boon romances. It is not until Beauty can feel love 'freely' and shed real tears that the beast can be transformed back into the man he is underneath. Her love will convert the potent sexuality into domestic bliss as in Mills and Boon, where male sexual aggression, usually exhibited by a moody, troubling indifference towards the heroine, will be tamed by love. Carter, therefore, consciously and ironically plays with the romance formula whereby troubling sexual difference is transformed through love into cosy domestication.

The heroine of 'The Tiger's Bridge', however, is a more knowing being both conscious and critical of her economic dependence on men:

I watched with the furious cynicism peculiar to women whom circumstances force mutely to witness folly, while my father, fired in his desperation by more and yet more draughts of the firewater they call 'grappa', rid himself of the last scraps of my inheritance.   (pp. 51–2)

The ironic narrative stance gives us a heroine with a consciousness capable of recognising directly her economic and sexual lack of freedom in a patriarchal world. Her father loses her to a tiger in a games of cards and the connection between materialism and sexuality is directly drawn. In giving her father a white rose at their parting, the heroine pricks her finger – 'and so he gets his rose all smeared with blood' (p. 55).

Ensconced in the tiger's palazzo, the heroine comes face to face with her own image in a 'clockwork twin' – a mechanical maid whom she will finally dress up in her own clothes and send back to her father to take her place. The tiger's only request is to see her naked, for which he will set her free and give her riches as a reward, but she refuses to subject herself to his gaze. It is not until he reveals himself naked to her that she complies, but simultaneously she realises she cannot be free within the patriarchal world her father inhabits:

> I was a young girl, a virgin, and therefore men denied me rationality just as they denied it to all those who were not exactly like themselves, in all their unreason. If I could see not one single soul in that wilderness of desolation all around me, then the six of us – mounts and riders, both – could boast amongst us not one soul, either, since all the best religions in the world state categorically that not beasts nor women were equipped with the flimsy, insubstantial things when the good Lord opened the gates of Eden and let Eve and her familiars tumble out. . . . I had been bought and sold, passed from hand to hand.   (p. 63)

Therefore the heroine's choice is between a father who values her only in market terms and a tiger, representative of a sexuality that is seemingly free from all economic interest. This is illustrated in the *dénouement* when the logic of the real animal world of the palazzo reasserts itself. By recognising her own sexuality the heroine finds 'liberty', and she sees that the tiger's sexual 'appetite need not be my extinction' (p. 67). The materiality of this world dissolves:

> And each stroke of his tongue ripped off skin after successive skin, all the skins of a life in the world, and left behind a nascent patina of shining hairs. My earrings turned back to water and trickled down my shoulders; I shrugged the drops off my beautiful fur.   (p. 67)

The question of choice, or lack of it, is echoed throughout the tales, and this is the Sadean framework – fuck or be fucked, both in the literal and in the metaphorical sense. Within this logic, to choose to fuck, given the options, seems a positive step, but the choice in fact is already prescribed. As Patricia Duncker puts it, 'we are watching . . . the ritual disrobing of the willing victim of pornography'.[7]

This comment is particularly applicable to the tale 'The Bloody Chamber', which begins,

> I remember how, that night, I lay awake in the wagon – lit in a tender, delicious ecstasy of excitement, my burning cheek

pressed against the impeccable linen of the pillow and the pounding of my heart mimicking that of the great pistons ceaselessly thrusting the train that bore me through the night, away from Paris, away from girlhood, away from the white enclosed quietude of my mother's apartment, into the unguessable country of marriage.   (p. 7)

The rhythm and language of this long sentence directly associates the movement of the train with the sexual anticipation of the adolescent heroine, with an imagination perhaps bred on Gothic horror stories. It is a tale full of Gothic motifs, and it plays with desire and danger, placing the reader, through the first-person narrative, in the heroine–victim position. This is the tale of one of Bluebeard's wives, and the heroine, seduced by wealth, power and mystery, skirts death in the quest for sexual knowledge. The narrative strategy, therefore, puts us the readers imaginatively within this ambivalent willing-victim position, and the tale attempts to illustrate not only the dangers of seduction, but also the workings of pleasure and danger seemingly implicit in sexuality for women. Again the narrative draws attention to the connection between material wealth and marriage. The heroine's mother has 'beggared herself for love' and thus tries to ensure her daughter's economic security by getting her a musical education. The heroine's corruption is threefold: material, as she is seduced by wealth; sexual, as she discovers her own sexual appetite; and moral, in the sense that 'like Eve' (p. 38) she disobeys her master–husband's command.

But this is a victim who is not only willing but also recognises that she has been bought:

This ring, the bloody bandage of rubies, the wardrobe of clothes from Poiret and Worth, his scent of Russian leather – all had conspired to seduce me so utterly that I could not say I felt one single twinge of regret for the world of tartines and maman that now receded from me as if drawn away on string, like a child's toy. . . .   (p. 12)

And, when she comes to pay the price, 'I guessed it might be so – that we should have a formal disrobing of the bride, a ritual from the brothels . . . my purchaser unwrapped his bargain' (p. 15). Her slow recognition of the real essence of the bargain she has struck is ironically underlined by the associations with death: 'A choker of rubies, two inches wide, like an extraordinarily precious slit throat' (p. 11); 'funereal lilies' (p. 9); and a husband with eyes 'dark and motionless as those eyes the ancient Egyptians painted upon their sarcophagi' (p. 12).

Her own sexual potential is another form of corruption. Again this is conveyed through contradictory impulses, and there is a sensual, physical detail in the writing:

> The perfume of the lilies weighed on my senses; when I thought that, henceforth, I would always share these sheets with a man whose skin, as theirs did, contained that toad-like, clammy hint of moisture, I felt a vague desolation that within me, now my female wound had healed, there had awoken a certain queasy craving like the cravings of pregnant women for the taste of coal or chalk or tainted food, for the renewal of his caresses. . . . I lay in bed alone. And I longed for him. And he disgusted me.
>
> (p. 22)

The intermingling of disgust and desire is not so much fear of the husband as for the sexuality in herself:

> I seemed reborn in his unreflective eyes, reborn in unfamiliar shapes. I hardly recognised myself from his descriptions of me and yet, and yet – might there not be a grain of beastly truth in them? And, in the red firelight, I blushed again, unnoticed, to think he might have chosen me because, in my innocence, he sensed a rare talent for corruption.   (p. 20)

The 'talent for corruption' is not only a willingness to be bought but also perhaps a willingness to participate in 'the thousand, thousand baroque intersections of flesh upon flesh' (p. 22), amply detailed in a connoisseur's collection of sado-masochistic volumes found in the library.

Of all the tales in the volume I found 'The Bloody Chamber' most troubling in terms of female sexuality, largely because of the very seductive quality of the writing itself. As readers we are asked to place ourselves imaginatively as masochistic victims in a pornographic scenario and to sympathise in some way with the ambivalent feelings this produces. The heroine's own subsequent recognition of total manipulation does not allay my unease at being manipulated by the narrative to sympathise with masochism. The writing playfully equivocates between explanation of the victims position and condemnation of the sadistic perpetrator of atrocities.

The husband puts the heroine to the test. He ostensibly goes away on business leaving her the keys to the castle with strict instructions not to enter his private room, which of course she does. There she discovers not only the mutilated bodies of his three former wives, but also the fate that awaits her. It seems, however, that the moral of the tale – that wives should not disobey their husbands – gets lost on the way, since as this quotation shows she had no choice in the matter anyway:

> The secret of Pandora's box; but he had given the box, himself, knowing I must learn the secret. I had played a game in which every move was governed by a destiny as oppressive and omnipotent as himself, since that destiny was himself; and I had lost. Lost at that charade of innocence and vice in which he had engaged me. Lost, as the victim loses to the executioner.
>
> (p. 34)

The husband promptly returns to claim his victim and what saves her is not the presence of the blind piano-tuner – he is merely a comfort – but her mother's prescience. Puzzled at her newly-wed daughter crying during a telephone call, she has intuitively recognised danger and flown to her rescue. Thus the *dénouement* gives us female revenge against male tyranny, but the heroine must wear the mark of her 'shame' on her forehead for ever. To be branded as guilty, despite recognition of the manipulation to which she has been subject, seems somewhat unfair. This is the only tale where the mother figure plays an important and positive role. In the others, as in their fairy-tale originals, mothers are either absent, insignificant or bad.

In the three tales described there is a foregrounding of the economic aspects of female sexuality in relation to patriarchy and thus an emphasis on the latent meaning of traditional tales. Patricia Duncker describes them in this way:

> The boys must be taught courage. The girls must be taught fear. For girls the critical metamorphosis is sexual, menstruation, puberty, marriage. For Sleeping Beauty the symbolic curse that comes upon her is puberty, the first shedding of blood, the curse that can only be redeemed by marriage, her rightful place. All

women have to do is wait. She must not initiate sexual activity, a potential she now possesses that is fraught with danger. She must wait and sleep out the years until she is possessed.[8]

In cultural terms, of course, virginity is the ultimate sign of female purity – it is a state with magical properties. Western civilisation has a religion founded on a miraculous virgin birth, and female sexuality defines female identity. This is outlined by Kirsten Hastrup:

> The first stage is that of the unspecified, yet creative virgin; the next stage is that of the sexually specified, child-bearing women, and the course is completed by a final return to unspecificity, this time of widowhood and of old women's impotence.[9]

Older women, therefore, move into a nebulous space where their potential for evil, as witches and hags, predominates over their potential for good, as fairy godmothers. Virgins are always susceptible to preying males who, if the young women are not careful, will take from them the thing of value they possess. As the heroine of 'The Tiger's Bride' observes, 'my own skin was my sole capital in the world and today I'd make my first investment' (p. 56). Sex outside marriage threatens the social order constructed through patriarchal fears over property and possessions, and fairy tales are very much concerned with the sexual economy. Most of the tales in *The Bloody Chamber* concentrate on the states of virginity and puberty. The only tale that deals specifically with a married female figure is 'Puss-in-Boots', which is a kind of Chaucerian fabliau told from the point of view of a salacious 'puss'. Here the female goes to adulterous fornication with gusto and with little concern for social niceties. Though amusing, the tale does not have much to recommend it in terms of sexual politics.

Another beast that rears its sexual head in various guises is the wolf, which features in the three short tales that close the volume: 'The Werewolf', 'The Company of Wolves' and 'Wolf Alice'. 'The Werewolf' is an appetiser for the others and is a variation on the story of Little Red Riding Hood. The moral is plain: 'The wolf may be more than he seems' (p. 111) – only in this case he is granny herself.

'The Company of Wolves' is another version of 'The Tiger's Bride'. 'Strong minded' Red Riding Hood wilfully sets off to visit granny while 'the malign door of the solstice swings upon its hinges', but in the 'pentacle of her own virginity' she fears nothing (p. 113). Meeting a handsome gentleman on the way, and failing to notice that 'gleaming trails of spittle clung to his teeth' (p. 114), she hopes he will reach granny's house first so that he can win the wager and gain a kiss. He does of course, treating granny as an *hors d'oeuvre* to Red Riding Hood's 'immaculate flesh' (p. 118). She recognises the danger but refuses to be a sacrificial victim: 'The girl burst out laughing; she knew she was nobody's meat. She laughed at him full in the face, she ripped off his shirt for him and flung it into the fire, in the fiery wake of her own discarded clothing' (p. 118). Thus, 'sweet and sound she sleeps in granny's bed, between the paws of the tender wolf' (p. 118). The point again is the acceptance of animal sexuality, but with a choice between rape and death such acceptance might seem merely logical rather than natural.

The third tale, however, inverts the second inasmuch as the 'wolf' is a girl child nurtured by wolves. She is rescued from the litter. Nuns try to civilise her but fail, and she ends up as a domestic servant to a werewolf. With a canine consciousness she tries to unravel the meaning of menstruation and budding sexuality. This process is simultaneous with a recognition of self in the mirror – a sort of Lacanian mirror phase moved to puberty: hence the 'Alice' of the title. In effect menstruation brings both a consciousness of time and awareness of a sexual identity, which manifests itself in her desire to put on an old dress and wander out into the world. The nurturing instincts that seemingly come with female sexuality are put to good use when her master returns home one night wounded: 'she was pitiful as her gaunt grey mother; she leapt upon his bed to lick without hesitation, without disgust, with a quick tender gravity, the blood and dirt from his cheeks and forehead' (p. 126). This tale suggests that sex and gender identity are one in the same. Even without cultural conditioning young women will want to put on dresses and minister to the sick in a maternal way. Nature has ascendancy over nurture.

Similarly, in 'The Erl-King' desire is the product of nature – the Erl-King 'came alive from the desire of the woods' (p. 86) – but we deduce from the punch-line, 'Mother, mother, you have murdered me!' (p. 91), that the Erl-King is also the created child of desire in an Oedipal configuration, and therefore potentially dangerous: 'Erl-King will do you grievous harm' (p. 85). Thus,

A young girl would go into the wood as trustingly as Red Riding Hood to her granny's house but this light admits of no ambiguities and, here, she will be trapped in her own illusion because everything in the wood is exactly as it seems. (p. 85)

Desire is dangerous because you may create out of it the cage of your own entrapment, like the young girls trapped as birds in the Erl-King's cages. I prefer 'The Snow Child', a short, sardonic piece on conflict between mother and daughter for the father's love, because, despite their story's reinforcement of the Electra complex and patent lack of sisterhood, the father's created child of desire literally melts away.

The elements of death and desire are also central to 'The Lady of the House of Love'. The Countess is part Sleeping Beauty, part descendant of Vlad the Impaler: 'she hovers in a no-man's land between life and death, sleeping and waking, behind the hedge of spiked flowers, Nosferatu's sanguinary rosebud' (p. 103). She has a 'horrible reluctance for the role' of vampire (p. 195) and desires to be human, to wake from her sleeping death like Sleeping Beauty woken by a single kiss. Here it is the virgin hero who is protected by his innocence. Patricia Duncker comments,

In fact what the Countess longs for is the grande finale of all 'snuff' movies in which the woman is sexually used and ritually killed, the oldest cliché of them all, sex and death. She can abandon her predatory sexuality, the unnatural force, as her own blood flows, the symbolic breaking of the virgin hymen, the initiation into sexual maturity and then into death.[10]

This seems to me apt but again ignores the irony: the Countess is the archetypal opposite of Sleeping Beauty and with a wistful pathos longs to be the fairy-tale figure she mimics, even though it will be the death of her. Desire yet again is dangerous.

In her 'Polemical Preface' to *The Sadeian Woman* Carter invokes history:

But our flesh arrives to us out of history, like everything else does. We may believe we fuck stripped of social artifice; in bed, we even feel we touch the bedrock of human nature itself. But we are deceived. Flesh is not an irreducible human universal. Although the erotic relationship may seem to exist freely, on its own terms, among the distorted social relationships of a bourgeois society, it is in fact the most self-conscious of all human relationships. . . .[11]

Therefore, Carter rightly argues, desire is a social construct and ideology shapes subjectivity but is itself subject to the historical process. In the 'wolf' tales, 'The Erl-King', 'The Snow Child' and 'The Lady of the House of Love', the economics of sexuality are abandoned for a concentration on the nature of desire and sexual subjectivity itself. Carter wants to explore boundaries and taboos in an anthropological rather than sociological vein and perhaps challenge certain feminist orthodoxies. But, divorced from the economic in 'The Company of Wolves', sexual choice becomes a question of straightforward survival in a seemingly natural, brutally physical male world. In 'Wolf Alice' sexual subjectivity becomes predetermined by sex alone, and in 'The Erl-King' desire is dangerous but precisely how is open to question. Sex is always and everywhere heterosexual. Desire *is* dangerous for women, for very good material reasons, and the romances of Mills and Boon put across messages about the protection of those interests in much the same way as fairy tales. Desire does not just exist in an unspecified way, but, as Carter points out in *The Sadeian Woman*, is ideologically and historically constructed. That her tales leave the nature of that constructedness out of the picture is somewhat of a disappointment.

Carter's treatment of fairy tales themselves is similar. By foregrounding their significance within her own tales Carter provides another layer of meaning. David Punter, analysing her novel *Heroes and Villains*, comments, 'Carter ironically suggests that the Gothic visions is in fact an accurate account of life, of the ways we project our fantasies onto the world and then stand back in horror when we see them come to life.'[12] This is also true of fairy tales. Thus, for the tiger's bride,

Old wives' tales, nursery fears! I knew well enough the reason for the trepidation I cosily titillated with superstitious marvels of my childhood on the day my childhood ended. For now my own skin was my sole capital in the world and today I'd make my first investment. (p. 56)

Nursery fears become made flesh and sinew; earliest and most archaic of fears, fears of devourment. . . . (p. 67)

The problem with Carter's attempts to foreground the relationship between fairy tales and reality, a productive exercise, is that the action for the heroines is contained within the same ideological parameters. So the actual constructedness of reality and the ideological premises of fairy tales remain intact. The tiger's bride, like the other heroines, realises the 'truth' of the 'nursery fears' and chooses a non-materialistic, animal sexuality, but she does not have the option of *not* choosing it. Within the framework of the tale her choice appears to be a liberating one, but in reality it is not, despite Carter's Sadean proposition that misogyny can be undermined by women's refusal to be sexual victims and by their adoption of a more sexually aggressive role.

Although there are dangers in comparing theoretical and fictional writing, I feel it is perfectly justifiable to argue that many of the ideas in *The Bloody Chamber* rest on Carter's interpretation of Sade, even if they do not fulfil her own analysis of the mechanisms of the historical process. It is possible to say that some of the tales 'render explicit the nature of social relations' as outlined in Carter's definition of the 'moral pornographer', but explanation is not always enough. Indeed, 'The Bloody Chamber' tale, through its equivocation, borders on the reactionary. We do have to address questions of binary thinking as it affects gender and sexuality, but Carter's prescribed action for her heroines within stereotypical options is ultimately politically untenable. Her use of irony might blur the boundaries at times but it does not significantly attack deep-rooted ways of thinking or feeling.

I began this essay by mentioning the collection of short stories *Wayward Girls and Wicked Women*. Unfortunately, the 'girls' in the tales of *The Bloody Chamber* can most often be designated 'wayward' – they do not value their virginity more than their lives; they get seduced by wealth; they cynically weigh their chances in a world full of male predators – and 'wicked women', rather thin on the ground, remain stereotypically wicked.

NOTES

1. A. Sebestyen, 'The Mannerist Marketplace', *New Socialist*, Mar 1987, p. 38.
2. Angela Carter, *The Bloody Chamber* (Harmondsworth: Penguin, 1981). Page references in text.
3. Angela Carter, *The Sadeian Woman* (London: Virago, 1979) pp. 19–20.
4. Ibid., p. 27.
5. Ibid.
6. Patricia Duncker, 'Re-imagining the Fairy Tales: Angela Carter's Chambers', *Literature and History*, Spring 1984, p. 6.
7. Ibid., p. 7.
8. Ibid., p. 9.
9. Kirsten Hastrup, 'The Semantics of Biology: Virginity', in S. Ardener (ed.), *Defining Females* (London: Croom Helm, 1978) p. 59.
10. Duncker, in *Literature and History*, Spring 1984, p. 9.
11. Carter, *The Sadeian Woman*, p. 9.
12. David Punter, *The Literature of Terror* (London: Longman, 1980) p. 398.

11
Sex and the Superman
An Analysis of the Pornographic Content of Marinetti's *Mafarka le futuriste*

CAROL DIETHE

The Superman whose coming was announced by Nietzsche to an incredulous reading public in *Thus Spoke Zarathustra* (1883–5) was destined to receive his most thorough literary characterisation in Marinetti's only full-length novel, *Mafarka le futuriste* (written in French and swiftly banned for obscenity when it appeared in Paris in 1909). This cannot be explained by any similarity between the two writers: Nietzsche was an academic and a recluse who was unsuccessful with women and never married, while Marinetti, rich and extrovert, thrived on publicity and eventually, after a turbulent youth, became a model paterfamilias. However, although Zarathustra and Mafarka may differ as literary characters, they are clearly linked in so far as Zarathustra is a prophet who preaches belligerent and misogynist ideas, and Mafarka is a rapacious warlord who puts these ideas into effect.

One central issue which unites Zarathustra and Mafarka is their belief that women deserve – and welcome – male sexual aggression. This view was held (in varying degree) by the male establishment at the turn of the century, so that Freud spoke openly of female masochism as the distinguishing feature of female sexuality,[1] and even doctors such as Mantegazza, who went out of their way to be fair-minded towards women, had to conclude that the sex act was simply a matter of aggression and defence.[2] This encouraged the assumption that the genteel wife and mother was sexless, whereas the woman with a pronounced sex drive was an aberration. The familiar Madonna-*versus*-Eve dichotomy was thus sustained by what can be termed 'received misogyny', which rested on a distorted view of female sexuality which many women, as well as men, accepted, although it was not entirely unchallenged.[3]

Fundamental to the distorted view of female sexuality was the belief that a woman's overriding instinct was to become pregnant, a view which led misogynist thinkers such as Weininger to warn that women were predators on the male sex rather than the other way round.[4] It is characteristic of many early-twentieth-century writers that they excuse or condone violence inflicted on women by stressing that the male is merely fighting off the vampiric female. This type of role reversal was given its fullest exposé as early as 1870 in Leopold von Sacher-Masoch's *Venus in Furs*, where the hero Severin (alias Sacher-Masoch) endures a variety of tortures at the hands of his mistress, Wanda – all, it must be noted, at his urgent request. Sacher-Masoch provides Severin with an escape route by means of a framework story in which he dreams that he becomes enslaved by the goddess Venus, naked except for a huge fur. She taunts Severin by saying, 'You [men of the Northern hemisphere] can only exorcise and curse me or sacrifice yourselves in bacchic frenzy at my altar.'[5]

The degraded existence which Severin leads during the novel has tempted one critic to describe it as 'the brutal reality of a totally submissive life',[6] which is to neglect the fact that the pain inflicted on Severin is an exquisite pleasure to him. Furthermore, since it was instigated by him in the first place it can be stopped at his behest. In other words, the pain itself is under male control even when Venus is invoked as arch-seductress or 'she-devil'. The pain inflicted sadistically on women in pornographic literature is *also* under male control, as we shall see in *Mafarka le futuriste*.

The whip which is so active a component in *Venus in Furs* is drawn into *Thus Spoke Zarathustra* with a quite different intention: that of subjugating women. Nietzsche wrote, 'Are you visiting women? Do you forget your whip' (*Zarathustra*, p. 93),[7] somewhat maliciously placing the words in the mouth of an old woman. According to Zarathustra, 'the true man wants two things: danger and play. For that reason he wants woman, as the most dangerous plaything' (p. 91). The siren in woman must be bridled: Eve must be taught to accept – indeed desire – her role as nurse to the warrior and mother to his offspring. 'Let your hope be: "May I bear the Superman!"' (p. 92).

Although Nietzsche trivialises the role of woman by making her man's 'plaything' (reminiscent of the rattle mentioned scathingly by Mary Wollstonecraft[8]), and makes constant jibes about pregnancy as the ideal method of keeping women docile, at the back of his mind there is always a serious acceptance of the necessity to procreate. In this respect his thinking is a continuation of Schopenhauer's, who believed that 'women in truth exist entirely for the propagation of the race'.[9] Schopenhauer included in his system a disembodied sexual libido as a facet of the 'will to live', which becomes in Nietzsche's hands the dynamo behind the 'will to power'. Sexual libido in the Superman is just one aspect of his turbulent energy.

By underwriting the importance of the role of mother, albeit in a roundabout way, Nietzsche – in spite of his apparent iconoclasm – endorsed the conventional view of the day regarding female sexuality. This is an aspect of his work which is often overlooked. He lost no time in pouring scorn on the emancipated woman: only man can be truly free to suffer, fight, laugh, dance in Dionysian ecstasy and love violently. Women are relegated to the position of brood mares: sex is for the Superman.[10]

Marinetti had an unusual upbringing. He was born to Italian parents in Alexandria, where he was brought up; he studied in Paris and Italy and came under the influence of D'Annunzio, Jarry and Apollinaire as well as of Nietzsche. He thus travelled light in comparison to Nietzsche, who never really escaped the stuffy conventions of Wilhelmine Germany, however much he attacked philistinism in his works. Marinetti enjoyed spending the fortune he had inherited from his father, and he loved foreign travel and excitement. His first erotic feelings were directed towards his African nurse, and his descriptions of the Africans in *Mafarka le futuriste* show sharp observation when, for example, superstitious beliefs are described. Another clear influence on the book is Marinetti's affection for his mother (which is echoed by Mafarka) and his love for his younger brother Leone, who died young (Mafarka's brother Magamal also dies young in the novel, much to Mafarka's chagrin).

Mafarka le futuriste thus strains, on occasion, to be something that it is not: Mafarka is credible when he is at his most cruel, especially towards women. Any relaxation of *machismo* on the part of Mafarka, as Superman, is a disruptive element in terms of the plot's coherence. Whereas, in Nietzsche's work, Zarathustra's mood changes are an integral part of the fabric of the book, any gentleness in the psychotic Mafarka sounds maudlin. Thus his concern for Ouarabelli-Charchar, Magamal's bride, ripped apart by her husband in his death throes (he has rabies), sounds out of place because it *is* out of place. Mafarka is actually much more distressed that his brother should be in such a state than that Ouarabelli-Charchar should die in such a horrible way. This is not to say that the book is without moments of convincing lyricism: indeed, the evocations of nature are central to the work. The whole realm of nature is described in pictoral and colourful interaction with the main characters – chiefly, of course, Mafarka, in what Marinetti promises in the Preface will be a polyphonic novel.

As the novel has not yet been translated into English[11] (Marinetti himself translated it into Italian), I shall give a résumé of the plot before analysing those aspects of Mafarka's sexuality which constitute the pornographic content of the novel. Mafarka-el-bar is the king of Tell-el-Kibir; his fortress lies close to the African sea-coast, and the sea is constantly mentioned in the novel. In its twelve chapters Mafarka's exploits are described in a chaotic manner: sometimes in minute detail and sometimes on a metaphysical level. Mafarka the warlord defeats his enemies both by prowess in war and by cunning, reminding us that in the same year as that in which the novel was printed, Marinetti also issued his first manifesto, *The Founding and Manifesto of Futurism* (1909), in which he declares war to be 'the world's only hygiene'.[12] These words are echoes verbatim in the Preface to the novel, and in the first chapter Mafarka chides his soldiers for indulging in mass rape when they ought to be fighting. In the second chapter, Mafarka infiltrates the enemy camp in disguise and tells the superstitious king, Brafane-el-Kibir, a series of obscene tales which stress Mafarka's own sexual potency. In the third chapter, the enemy unleash a huge pack of rabid hounds on Mafarka's fortress. Although Mafarka has invented a machine which he calls a 'war giraffe', because it is built in the shape of a giraffe, with a sprung neck that can throw large missiles a long distance, the end result is that Magamal is bitten by one of the dogs. His death is 'the price of victory' (the title of the fourth chapter). Mafarka's bloodlust is not confined to the battlefield. In an underground cave he has constructed a huge aquarium filled with predatory fish; he amuses his friends by feeding two of his enemies to the sharks. Ignoring the protests of his friends, he orders two belly-dancers to be despatched in the same way, an incident to which we shall return.

Magamal's horrific death retains its capacity to shock the reader because Mafarka insists upon carrying the corpse round with him in a hippopotamus hide and actually kills two treacherous sailors by dealing them blows with it. Before killing a third traitor, Mafarka removes the rigid body from the hide in order to invoke the dead Magamal's aid. Mafarka's grief over his brother's death actually forms the core of three chapters (4, 6 and 7), and in the eighth chapter Mafarka seeks out his mother's spirit among the tombs. He decides to placate his mother's anger over what he construes to be his own negligence towards Magamal by building a mechanical, and hence immortal, son. When his subjects plead with him to return to the throne, Mafarka rejects them with the blunt message, 'you can tell them all that I have become an engineer of mechanical birds' (*Mafarka*, p. 211).[13] The son is to be a giant metamorphosed aeroplane.

Mafarka has Gazourmah constructed out of metal and, summoning all his will power and appealing to the sun and the earth for strength, he breathes life into his creation, which, flicking its creator to his death, comes into being noisily, fulfilling the novel's opening promise of polyphony with 'the great dream of total music' (p. 305). Inspired by Nietzsche's insistence that music was the most sublime of the arts, and probably also by Mahler's *Song of the Earth*, Gazourmah's maiden flight represents the pinnacle of earthly achievement: 'The flight of all the songs of the earth were completed in the great beating of his inspired wings' (p. 306). The birth of Gazourmah occurs during a cosmic storm which, if it were not on such a colossal scale, would have much in common with the description of the birth of the monster in Mary Shelley's *Frankenstein* (1818). The earth is convulsed in a dance of death: the mountains take on human characteristics, suffering and dying while the sea rages, and the sun is ordered, by Gazourmah, to retreat, 'deposed king whose kingdom I have destroyed!' (*Mafarka*, p. 305).

The events of the novel are extraordinary enough without the stylistic component which makes the novel breathless, ecstatic and at times rhapsodic. Mafarka, with Marinetti's obvious approval, is a man in a hurry: a Superman with a large appetite for life and a notorious sex drive. Mafarka has an inordinately long penis which, according to the tale which he tells the enemy Brafane-el-Kibir (whilst in disguise as a beggar), grew when he ate his stallion's severed penis, which a wicked demon had served up to him as a supposed delicacy. Given the almost sacred status accorded to the male organ in this novel, one might have expected Mafarka to vomit up the meal when he discovered that it was not the exotic fish he had been led to believe, just as Thyestes vomited up the flesh of his children when it was served to him in a pie. Not so Mafarka: the brute strength of his stallion, distilled in the penis, increases his potency so that he immediately pounces on the servants girls, all of whom, it must be noted, enjoy being ravished. By this time, Mafarka's penis has become so extended that it is a severe encumbrance:

> Having satiated himself on about twenty servants and almost as many pretty female slaves, Mafarka-el-bar, feeling dead tired, desired to sleep in the fresh sea air and had a soft couch placed on the terrace which jutted out over the mole of the port. . . . Mafarka stretched out his body voluptuously on it, but his interminable penis, which measured eleven cubits, was too cumbersome! . . . So he hit on the idea of coiling it up carefully like a cable at the foot of the couch; having done this he fell into a deep sleep. It so happened that the next morning a sailor whose eyes were still sleepy mistakenly took the member for a rope and attached it firmly to a jib sail. Then he threw the lot over the parapet to the sailors who were on the bow of a sailing ship. The latter started to pull in rhythm, shouting: – Heave-ho! . . . Heave-ho! – to clew up the sail. Immediately the penis, enormous because of an erection, rose high and unfurled the jib sail which filled with wind with a clap. And Mafarka, still sleeping, was thus transported on a gentle flight, sailing over the sea billows with his erect penis like a vibrating mast, beneath the sail which was filled with a favourable breeze.   (pp. 64–5)

It comes as no surprise that the warrior Mafarka should regard his penis as a weapon. The notions of love and death are inextricably linked throughout the novel, so that Mafarka's natural response to two young girls who look at him, full of admiration and desire, is to tell them, 'what I relish most about you is the desire to kill you! What can you expect of a living dagger such as I?' (p. 120). This component of sadism is a common feature of pornography; it is clearly found in de Sade's *Justine* (1791), where the link between pleasure and pain is explored in depth.[14] One must bear in mind that pornography by its very definition treats women as sex objects, so that, even in a book such as *Venus in Furs*, where the woman appears, literally, to have the whip hand, this applies only as long as it suits the male protagonist, as already discussed.

It is also assumed in pornographic literature – and *Mafarka* is no exception – that women are at a constant high peak of desire and that, to put it bluntly, rape does them good. This assumption enables the writer (nearly always male) to make light of any resistance on the woman's part. The argument can be traced in a clear line of development in the following extract from the rape scene in *Mafarka*, where the initial resistance of the women is brutally mastered so that – though they are chained on their backs by a stagnant pool whilst hundreds of naked warriors line up to rape them – the description of pain gives way to that of pleasure:

> One could see the smooth shiny bellies of the young women and their little breasts the colour of burnt coffee twisting in anguish under the heavy fists of the males, whose bronze loins rose and fell indefatigably amongst the agitated and crackling green putrefaction.
>
> Some of the men were singing mournful recitative chants, others furiously bit into their mistresses' hair, then stopped, their mouths full of bloody hair, and remained kneeling for a long time staring at those pitiable eyes revulsed with grief, horror and lust.
>
> For they [the women] sometimes bounded with a pleasure more bitter because it was involuntary under the reflex of a strong spasm. . . .
>
> The youngest of them, of an elegant, pliant and unhealthy beauty, was called Biba. Her whole body, contorted with hysteria, clung to her lover like a damp cloth and responded with violent jolts to the deep blows dealt to her by the penis minute by minute . . . and each time she let out screams of anguished joy, so shrill and rending that they pierced and dominated the uproar of the sonorous ravine. Her raucous purple voice dolefully implored for embrace: 'Mahmoud, oh Mahmoud, kill me, kill me like this. Oh! You're killing me with hot pleasure! You're filling my pussy's mouth with sugar and hallaouha. It is so pleasant to be gorged with titbits like that!'
>
> (pp. 30–2)

Marinetti reinforces the vocabulary of male aggression throughout the book by making the women speak of their own sexuality in demeaning terms. The animal imagery which has been used so effectively to establish Mafarka as a stud is constantly employed to reduce women to simpering kittens, partly, it must be noted, because the obscene French words for the female genitalia have a similar sense to the English 'pussy'. Hence Biba's allusion to her own orgasm as a treat for her 'pussy' deflects attention away from the bestiality of the action taking place, so that Marinetti feels at ease to crack jokes, having once established that the women are responding voluptuously, if involuntarily, to the rape.

Although Biba is creating a noise, the silence of most of the women annoys the men, who attack the women from a different position in order to cause merriment among the spectators:

> then they fell back heavily flat on their stomachs and buried their mouths in the hollow of the vulva, which they lapped noisily like dogs whilst they made their legs kick about in the mud to splash the spectators squatting on the bank, whose gaiety redoubled.   (p. 32)

Although at first sight the dog imagery sounds almost as demeaning as the cat vocabulary, it is used in a context where male power is being exercised, and reinforces the blind might of the 'dogs of war'. It also provides a forward reference to the rabid dogs of chapter 3, 'The Sun Dogs'. In addition, the grotesque humour whereby female anatomy is reduced to a dog's feeding-bowl establishes the women as inanimate objects and leads up to their final degradation, where they are sunk as boats. One of the warriors, nicknamed 'Prick-el-Kibir' because of his genital credentials, decides to hold a macabre regatta:

> Let everyone mount on board his mistress. I already have mine under my belly, and I'm sailing very well; my oar is solid . . . Oh! how one scuds along! Look! my black barge is going to sink . . . she is almost invisible . . . It's because of this terrible speed. . . . Let's give a prize to the person who kills his dinghy before everyone else! Allah! Mine won't budge! . . . Never mind! It must get going again! . . . There, it's gliding, it's gliding! . . .
>
> (pp. 33–4)

This offensive passage is followed by a general description of the pond, which becomes a writhing bloody mass as the massacre takes its course. What could conceivably have been read as an ironic discourse on mindless sexuality becomes, through the constant inclusion of sadistic detail, a sustained pornographic indulgence on Marinetti's part, and the end result is the opposite of erotic.

As already pointed out, a fundamental feature of pornographic literature is that it uses women as sexual objects. It has also been established in this essay that a fundamental feature of the Superman is his unthinking brutality, which in the case of Marinetti's Mafarka receives full authorial approval. The mixture of sex and Superman is thus an automatic crucible waiting only for the women to be added before the sadistic explosion occurs. If the women can be shown to welcome the rapacious approaches of the Superman, this greatly adds to his image as potent male. Thus, in the scene where Mafarka's penis becomes elongated through his ingestion of the stallion's penis, the ravished girls echo the equine vocabulary, and their hilarity gives the scene an overlay of legitimacy:

> Then Mafarka pounced on the young servant girls who were clearing the table and threw them down on the cushions, one after another, laughing like a madman. And they laughed too and cried out in turn: 'Oh . . . , my lovely steed, just bury your head in my little manger! Ah! . . . just your head . . . Yes! . . . Oh! . . .'   (pp. 62–3)

Mafarka himself makes constant use of the feline vocabulary discussed above in order to demonstrate the superior brandishing vigour of the rampant male:

> Oh! I know how to go to work then, rubbing firmly between women's thighs and knocking on their pretty little hole to kill with great blows of my prick the irritated cat which stretches its limbs, miaows, yawns, licks its coat and burns all around it with its breath!   (p. 120)

Gradually, however, a change takes place: Mafarka's misogyny becomes increasingly virulent and the cat imagery is no longer sufficient. Women are referred to as spiders (because some spiders eat the male), as sorceresses, and the word 'vulva' is continually used as a term of abuse. Twice Mafarka breaks off in the middle of intercourse because he finds that the woman is enjoying it too much (pp. 234 and 245). This male suspicion of the woman's sexual enjoyment is a recidivist aspect of the Superman, reminding us of Nietzsche's view, which was shared by many of his contemporaries, that women are dangerous: none more so than the sexually active Eves.

Mafarka, whose every action is exaggerated, takes his fear of the sexually eager woman to psychotic lengths. In the fifth chapter, Mafarka, irritated by the erotically suggestive dance of the belly-dancers, forces them to compromise themselves and then has them thrown to the sharks. He has the cave darkened so that nothing can be seen, and orders the two dancers to smell out the most vile man present: 'That's the game! You choose following your nostrils, or better still the instinct of your vulva because your eyes might trip you up and you could be taken in by the finery of my dress' (p. 146). It is clear from this passage that Mafarka knows that the girls will choose him: he is thus setting a deliberate trap for them. This does not prevent him from evincing horrified surprise when one of the girls smells him out:

> Curse! Damnation! . . . Like butterflies and flies, you have invisible tubes to suck up the strength and odour of the male! . . . Like female spiders, you make yourselves up to look like rosebuds and you even give off intoxicating scents to attract insects like us who are choosy with flowers! . . . You cover yourselves with scales so that you look like the sea sparkling in the sun, and our desire for brilliancy makes us your victim! . . . You cover yourselves with tinkling objects, because tigers are charmed by means of a little bell! . . . All the poison of hell is in your glances and the saliva of your lips has a lustre which kills . . . yes, which kills just as well and better than daggers!
>
> (p. 147)

The scene with the belly-dancers is central not only because it comes almost halfway through the book: it also prepares the reader for Mafarka's emotional breakdown which will result from Magamal's death. This death forces him to consider – and reject – the necessity of mortality. He knows that he himself will die but is obsessed with the idea of building a mechanical replacement for Magamal. The vocabulary of sexuality becomes increasingly confused because Mafarka now becomes intent on discrediting women as child-bearers in general. In this sense, the titanic Mafarka breaks away from the Nietzschean Superman. He is also deviant in not accepting the doctrine of 'eternal recurrence' which lies at the heart of *Thus Spoke Zarathustra*. This doctrine could have brought solace to Mafarka, because it teaches that 'time itself is a circle . . . all things have been here before' (*Zarathustra*, p. 178). Magamal would thus return to earth in exactly the same form.

In a sense, the Mafarka of the earlier chapters is more accessible to the reader: however unpleasant his exploits, he is the paradigmatic Superman. The Mafarka of the later chapters abdicates his role as Superman to the robot Gazourmah, and the book loses much of its dynamism, in spite of Gazourmah's bravado. In addition, the reader is caused a good deal of confusion by Mafarka's (and possibly Marinetti's) conflicting attitudes towards the mother figure, who is given a sanctified status at one level (the ghost of Mafarka's mother, Langourama) but vilified on another level in the character of Coloubbi.

Coloubbi is simultaneously the spirit of Mafarka's youth – his demon who knows when he will die – and an earthly woman who seeks to enchant Mafarka with her physical attributes. Coloubbi represents the maternal principle in the novel: she merges Eve with Madonna by being an enticingly beautiful woman who wishes to ensnare the male so that her destiny as child-bearer can be fulfilled. Mafarka feels threatened by Coloubbi because she might deflect his determination to build an immortal creation. In a sense, Mafarka's fears are justified, because Coloubbi does try to lay claim on Gazourmah. Because Mafarka interrupts intercourse with her, and thus robs her of the chance of being impregnated, she maliciously seeks to corrupt Gazourmah by gazing at him voluptuously during his inception. After his creation, Coloubbi asserts that she is both Gazourmah's mistress and his mother. She tells Mafarka,

> He's my son, you know, from the moment his first glance was for me! . . . I melted with pleasure under the rough caress of his eyes! . . . He's also my lover, and I surrendered myself to all his caprices in that first look! . . . You see, all by myself I get a terrible pleasure from his male power – he who is already dreaming of killing me by emptying his veins into mine! . . .
> (p. 283)

Coloubbi's masochistic desire for a *Liebestod* is brought to fruition when she commits suicide by hurling herself at Gazourmah's metal breast while he watches her suffering, trembling 'with cruel joy' (p. 300). Her death ushers in an apocalyptic tone in the final passages of the novel, because she is elevated to the status of Earth Mother. Gazourmah, by participating in her destruction, brings about a state of cosmic collapse which serves to inflate his own position as a new power in the universe.

Mafarka's rejection of Coloubbi does not occur without a good deal of reluctance on his part, because he does find her attractive. It is in her persona as earthly woman that Mafarka rejects any aspect of Coloubbi which might remind him that she could bear a child; he is particularly angered when she offers him her breast as part of a sexual advance: 'Oh! don't make my mother's gesture! . . . Your breasts are cursed and shrivelled! . . . Go away!' (pp. 251–2). The rejection of Coloubbi is a necessity if Mafarka is to allow his project to flourish, and Marinetti makes Mafarka's language towards women change to reflect the alteration in his own attitude. There is no more bantering over 'pussies': instead, Mafarka mounts a sustained attack on the female genital organs. He announces to his subjects,

> Know that I have given birth to my son without recourse to the vulva! . . . It is possible to grow a giant with invincible wings from one's own flesh without the competition and disgusting participation of the womb of woman! You must believe in the absolute and definitive power of the will which must be cultivated, intensified, following a cruel discipline, until the moment when it springs out of our nervous centres and throws itself beyond the limits of our muscles with an inconceivable power and speed.
>
> Our will must leave us in order to seize matter and modify it to our whim. In this way we can mould everything that surrounds us and renew the face of the earth without limit. Soon, if you ask it of our will, you will give birth without recourse to woman's vulva.   (pp. 214–15)

The three pejorative references to female anatomy in this brief extract indicate the extent of Marinetti's confusion of purpose. In order to elevate the machine-making Superman he is forced to degrade woman, but he is reluctant to relinquish the sexual vocabulary which has sustained the book to this point. The world of nature is now invoked to provide the sexual theme. Mafarka uproots a forest of trees to burn as an offering to the wind, and the whole bonfire is described in terms of love and lust. In fact,

Mafarka actually places the tree-trunks in couples 'so that they could bite each other better under the caress of the flame' (p. 261). After Mafarka's death, Gazourmah speaks to the breezes in a similar vein:

> like a tired lover slides out of the bed of an exhausted woman, that's how I shall fly! . . . I shall lean on you fearlessly because the more my speed increases, the more you will press your bodies down on my flying belly in the hope of stopping me by a greater resistance. Your voluptuous host will be at its most dense where I have passed through, because my brutal caresses will make you flow backwards in swirls. That's how water rises in front of the ship which cuts through it! . . . In order to inhale my male odour once more you will all rush back into the void which I shall leave behind, dispersing the whole voluptuous pack of you.   (pp. 298–9)

Although Marinetti has been at some pains to stress that Gazourmah is fitted with an enormous metal penis, sexual language such as that in the passage above sounds particularly absurd even in a tale which has so little tangential connection with reality. The harem of women surrounding Mafarka in the earlier chapters of the book make the frequent reference to intercourse seem part of the Superman's daily life, but the description of Gazourmah's penis sounds all the more grotesque because, like Frankenstein's monster, he is without a mate. Mafarka ignores this when he tells Gazourmah, 'I have finished my creation by chaining all the vertebrae in a supple column so that your strength can rush through to your superb bronzed member which will be able to dig deeply into the hot, moist down of virgins!' (p. 282). It is at this point that Gazourmah catches sight of Coloubbi and begins to spring into life – the first sign of this being, we are told, that 'Gazourmah's bent copper penis stiffened like a sword' (pp. 282–3).

Thus Marinetti continues to use the language of sexual violence and male dominance through to the end of the book, culminating in Gazourmah's sadistic treatment of Coloubbi and his rhapsodic flight, which constitutes a *tour de force* of ecstatic destruction. As stated at the outset, the element of sexual violence is what makes the novel dynamic according to its own precepts and pornographic according to those of society. The question remains: does that matter? After all, the book was banned; it cannot be said to have done any harm. However, this was not the only thing written by Marinetti, though it was the most offensive. He was, it must be remembered, the founder of Futurism, which, though it has its amusing and educative facets, also contained a deep grain of fascism, which Mussolini was quick to recognise and exploit. It also persuaded some people, notably Valentine de Saint-Point, to act against their own interest in rejecting feminism. Saint-Point tried to argue in favour of free love in her *Futurist Manifesto of Lust* (1913), but elsewhere her arguments in favour of female brutality – to equal male brutality – sound particularly unpleasant in the light of the events which were to follow, notably two disastrous world wars:

> don't let's have any feminism. Feminism is a political error. Feminism is a fault in woman's brain which her instinct will soon recognise. You cannot give women any of the rights demanded by the feminists.
>
> . . . May woman find her cruelty, her violence again to let loose on the vanquished because he is vanquished, so she can cripple him. Let people stop preaching about her spiritual sense of fair play which she tries in vain to acquire. Women, be noble, unjust like nature itself!
>
> . . . Women, you have been moral and prejudiced for too long: return to your noble instincts, to wildness and cruelty. Whilst the men fight and make war, make children as a bloody tribute to war and heroism . . . let them grow up to blossom in boundless freedom, not just to please you. You create them. You can do anything with them. You owe humanity heroes. So – produce them![15]

Mussolini and his ally Hitler must have been barely able to believe their luck that there were women prepared to put out such ideas. Marinetti became something of a fading star after the First World War, but he never rounded on Mussolini (who treated him somewhat shabbily) and he never publicly distanced himself from fascism. Indeed he renewed his link with Germany, which had inspired his early admiration for the Superman, when he attended a banquet given by the Nazis in his honour in 1933. By then, the ideas of the belligerent Superman seemed entirely in keeping with

National Socialist propaganda, as did Marinetti's idea that war is hygienic, although one must add immediately that the Nazi interpretations of Zarathustran 'lust for power' are perversions not to be found in Nietzsche, who regarded himself as a good European.

NOTES

1. A theme first raised by Freud in *Three Essays on the Theory of Sexuality* (1905) and elaborated upon in many subsequent works: for example, *The Economic Problem in Masochism* (1924), *Female Sexuality* (1931) and *The Psychology of Women* (1932, based on an earlier piece written in 1915–17).
2. Mantegazza, it must be noted, deplored the aggression of the male: 'Our Western civilization approaches woman like animals in heat, with hardly more than an animal comprehension of the anatomy and human refinements' – P. Mantegazza, *Sexual Relations of Mankind* (New York, 1935) p. 257. First published in Italian in 1892.
3. See Peter Gay, *The Bourgeois Experience*, 2 vols (New York and Oxford: Oxford University Press, 1984 and 1986) vol. ɪ, p. 153.
4. See Otto Weininger, *Sex and Character* (London and New York: Heinemann, 1906). First published in German in 1903.
5. Leopold von Sacher-Masoch, *Venus in Furs* (London: Sphere, 1969) p. 9.
6. Franz Kuna, *Kafka: Literature as Corrective Punishment* (London: Paul Ellek, 1974) p. 36.
7. Friedrich Nietzsche, *Thus Spoke Zarathustra*, tr. R. J. Hollingdale (Harmondsworth: Penguin, 1961). Page references in text. First published in German, 1883–92.
8. Mary Wollstonecraft, *Vindication of the Rights of Woman* (1792; Harmondsworth: Penguin, 1983) p. 118.
9. Arthur Schopenhauer, 'On Women', in *Essays of Schopenhauer*, tr. Mrs Rudolph Dirchs (London and Felling-on-Tyne: The Walter Scott Press, 1910) p. 70. First published in German in 1841.
10. For example, in *Ecce Homo* (written 1888, first published 1908), section 5: 'Why I Write Such Excellent Works'.
11. An omission I hope to remedy in the near future with my translation of the work. All translations from the novel in this essay are my own.
12. Umbro Apollonio (ed.), *Futurist Manifestos*, tr. Robert Brain, R. W. Flint, J. C. Higgitt and Caroline Tisdall (London: Thames and Hudson, 1973) p. 22.
13. F. T. Marinetti, *Mafarka le futuriste* (Paris, 1909). Page references in text. In quotations, Marinetti's suspension points (...) are set close together to distinguish them from ellipses (. . .) marking omissions.

14. There is nothing new in the notion that pleasure and pain are linked: it was familiar to the ancients, for example in the myth of Psyche and Eros.
15. Valentine de Saint-Point, 'Manifesto of the Futurist Woman', translated from *Der Sturm*, May 1912.

Index